Cold War Soldier

Cold War Soldier

Life on the Front Lines of the Cold War

Terry "Stoney" Burke

DUNDURN
TORONTO

Editor: Jennifer McKnight
Design: Jesse Hooper
Printer: Webcom

Library and Archives Canada Cataloguing in Publication

Burke, Terry, 1947-
    Cold War soldier : life on the front lines of the Cold War / written by Terry "Stoney" Burke.

Issued also in electronic format.
ISBN 978-1-55488-959-4

    1. Burke, Terry, 1947-. 2. Soldiers--Canada--Biography. 3. North Atlantic Treaty Organization--Armed Forces--Biography. 4. Cold War--History. I. Title.

U55.B87A3 2011   355.092   C2011-902584-1

1   2   3   4   5   15   14   13   12   11

We acknowledge the support of the **Canada Council for the Arts** and the **Ontario Arts Council** for our publishing program. We also acknowledge the financial support of the **Government of Canada** through the **Canada Book Fund** and **Livres Canada Books**, and the **Government of Ontario** through the **Ontario Book Publishing Tax Credit** and the **Ontario Media Development Corporation**.

Care has been taken to trace the ownership of copyright material used in this book. The author and the publisher welcome any information enabling them to rectify any references or credits in subsequent editions.

J. Kirk Howard, President

Printed and bound in Canada.
www.dundurn.com

Dundurn	Gazelle Book Services Limited	Dundurn
3 Church Street, Suite 500	White Cross Mills	2250 Military Road
Toronto, Ontario, Canada	High Town, Lancaster, England	Tonawanda, NY
M5E 1M2	LA1 4XS	U.S.A. 14150

Dedicated to Molly and Bill with love and unending respect

Contents

Introduction

Prelude to a Life

Dublin, Ireland, in the latter part of the 1950s was, without doubt, a wonderful place to grow up. The city and its suburbs presented unending opportunities for curious kids to explore. From our house at the western edge of the city, it was just a short walk in almost any direction to find adventure. Just up the street were the rail yards and the waters of the Grand Canal, running parallel along the northern edge of the city. Eddie Murphy, Al Kennedy, and I would stand atop the stone wall on the bridge looking down into the deep cold waters of the canal, daring each other to jump. Pass beyond the narrow stone canal bridge and you were in the country, with vast open fields and pasture land as far as the eye could see.

Less than a hundred yards off to the right stood a solitary abandoned mansion. Although we all believed the story about the ghosts that inhabited the place, it did not stop us from heaving rocks at the walls and shattering window frames every time we passed by. Eddie Murphy actually walked to the top on the veranda once, as the rest of us stood well back at a safe distance. No sooner had he taken a step toward the door when the wind caused the loose boards to clatter, sending all of us running for our lives back to the main road.

I always looked forward to spring, when my brothers and I would head out to the fields in search of berries. My mother would give each of us a large tin can and we spent the day scouring the bush lines along the dirt tracks and farmers' fields trying to be the first to fill the can with big, fat blueberries. By late that evening, the sweet smell of cooking blueberries would permeate the whole house, as my mother and sisters made jam for our next day's breakfast.

Long summer days were spent rambling through Phoenix Park. No trip home from the park was complete without first climbing the hedge row surrounding Primrose Orchards and filling our pockets with stolen apples.

The only real dark cloud in our young lives was the onset of fall and the start of another terrifying year at St Finbar's Catholic Boy's School. Our teacher priests were very adept in the use of the bamboo cane. Not a day went by without at least half of the class being whipped across the legs or arms. If the cane wasn't readily available, they were just as handy with a slap to the head or a swift kick to the backside. I can't speak for any of my brothers, who attended this institution longer than I, but in my two years there I learned very little other than an abiding fear of Catholic priests.

Even at age nine I knew our family was not "well off," but we were not what one would consider poor, either. My father struggled six days a week at a low-paying, back-breaking job. My eight brothers and sisters and I had a roof over our heads and we never went hungry. Our clothes may have been hand-me-downs, but we were always clean.

Except for school, life for us kids was simple and happy.

What we didn't know was that this simple childhood existence would come to an abrupt end for each of us at age sixteen. In the Ireland of the 1950s the unwritten rule was harsh but very straight forward: "You grow up to be what your father was."

Dad had worked hard as a labourer at the gas company his entire adult life, and he knew full well that this was the life for which his boys were destined if we remained in Ireland.

In the upcoming years, my father and I would grow far apart — based mostly on my becoming an intolerable little shit — but I never lost respect for what he had done for us. It must have taken tremendous courage for a man already past fifty to uproot his entire family and move them halfway around the world just to ensure his nine kids had a chance at a better life.

Throughout the first half of the twentieth century, Ireland's single largest export was human beings. Our large family became part of this sad statistic on an extremely hot and muggy day in June 1957, when we boarded the train in Dublin and headed for Shannon Airport and the long flight to Toronto, Canada.

After a short stay in a three-room flat on Dupont Street, we moved to an old, run down house at Dermott Place, right in the heart of Cabbagetown. The vast majority of our neighbours were either Italian or Irish, with a sprinkle of Eastern Europeans thrown into the mix. Being Catholic was the one thing most of us had in common. When we were not fighting amongst ourselves, there were always the gangs from Regent Park with which to contend. People used to say that you could come out of Cabbagetown one of two ways: either as a priest or an axe murderer. Most of my friends were inclined toward the latter.

The bad memories of those early school years were quickly fading. Shortly after we arrived in Toronto's east end, we were enrolled in St Martin's School and discovered, to our surprise, that we were somewhat more advanced than the other kids in our grades. I certainly had never been a straight-A student, but I had managed to maintain an above average grade level, at least in those early years.

By the start of Grade 8 we had moved up to the north end of the city, and my downhill spiral had begun. Things only got worse as I entered high school. I could try to blame it on many things, but the facts were simple: I was just lazy, and, having once again to deal with a steady string of teaching priests, I had lost all interest. Being sandwiched between two siblings who both achieved exceptionally good grades only made things worse, especially in the eyes of my father.

Being brought home by the police for everything from smoking on the street, to shoplifting, to getting into fist fights became almost a regular routine. Even when my father gave me a well-deserved wallop, I would briefly show some regret for my behaviour, but within days or even hours, I could shrug it off and go back to being the same incorrigible little shit.

On a Sunday evening in late September 1962, it all came to a sudden tragic end. In a matter of just minutes, all of our lives were abruptly changed forever. Nothing would ever be the same again.

My parents had spent the weekend shopping in Buffalo, New York, along with my sister and her husband. On the return trip, late that Sunday night, my brother in law had gotten lost, but eventually found his way back on to the Queen Elizabeth Way. As he attempted to turn back onto the highway, the car was struck broadside, killing my mother instantly.

My mother had been the stabilizing influence in our family. She had been the one that you went to when you were in trouble or when you just needed advice or a sympathetic ear. She had never been big "hugger," but we always knew that we were loved, even if the word itself was rarely used. On the frequent occasions when I had gotten myself into trouble, she would quietly listen and then send me upstairs to wait for my father to arrive home. She would act as the calming influence and talk to my father before he came up the stairs to see you. Dad was not averse to giving us a good wallop when it was necessary and, in my case, especially in those early teenage years, it was always well-deserved.

My father had worked extremely hard all his life. At the gas works in Dublin, he had done the back-breaking job of shovelling coal for ten to twelve hours a day. After we got to Canada, life didn't get any easier. Because he was already over fifty, there was little choice other than to take yet another low-paying labourer's job, working nights for the City roads' department. Despite the low pay and long, mind-numbing hours he worked, I never heard him complain.

On the rare occasions when he didn't have to work, he would pile us all onto a streetcar and head for Kew Beach. He would often embarrass my mother on one of these outings by striking up a conversation with a complete stranger. Within seconds he would have the wallet out to proudly display the accordion folder of family photos he always carried. My father smiled a lot in those early days. He called my mother "Mol," which was short for Molly. Although they were not very demonstrative in front of us kids, I know they loved each other a lot, simply by the way they looked at and spoke to each other. After my mother died, he rarely smiled again.

Just after my sixteenth birthday, I was in trouble with the law yet again. I had been brought home by the police for shoplifting, smoking on the street at the age of twelve, and once for sneaking into the movies without paying, but this time was much more serious, because now, at least in the eyes of the law, I was an adult and would be treated as such by the court. I spent a week in the Don Jail, on remand for stealing from Eaton's.

After seven days of absolute terror, I finally went back to court at the Old City Hall in downtown Toronto.

I remember the holding cell under the courthouse. It consisted of one large room, rectangular in shape, with bars on one side and three walls of greyish peeling paint. In the corner there was a toilet bowl with vomit on the seat, along with evidence of previous occupants' dried puke on the wall, and pools of urine surrounding the entire area. The stench of the twenty or so men in this cell, added to the smell of urine and vomit, was almost overwhelming.

Finally my name was called and I was escorted up a set of stairs to find myself in a small enclosure in the middle of the courtroom. A rather rumpled-looking man in his thirties approached and identified himself as a legal aid lawyer and warned me that, although I was likely to be sentenced to probation and allowed to go home today, there was a problem. No one in my family had come to speak for me, and the judge may not let me go without my father or some adult taking responsibility for me. After a lengthy discussion at the front of the court, most of which I could barely hear or understand, the judge called me forward, had me sworn in, and started to pepper me with questions about my crime. Why wasn't I in school, and did I realize how much of a disgrace I was to my family? I honestly thought my heart was going to pop right out of my chest. I could hear my own pulse pounding in my ears. I had trouble trying to catch my breath. Each response was met with annoyance from the judge and repeated orders to "Speak Up!"

Fortunately, my older brother Michael arrived and the judge released me with the warning that should he see me in his court again, I would not be going home for a very long time. The only advice Michael gave me on the long ride home was to be invisible and stay out of Da's way as long as possible. This turned out to be quite easy, because my father acted like I wasn't even there. He didn't speak to me, he didn't look at me — it was as if I didn't exist.

After an excruciating week, he finally broke the silence. He was putting on his coat, ready to leave for work at about four in the afternoon, when he walked into the living room and just stared at me for a few moments. His words were short and to the point: "You're sixteen now and I don't want you here anymore. Be out of this house by the time I get home from work tomorrow morning." That was all. Nothing more needed saying. I was a complete disappointment to him.

By early evening I had made my way back down to Cabbagetown and was heading for the Satellite Restaurant on Parliament Street where I hoped to run into some of my friends from the old neighborhood.

I sat at the restaurant counter for about an hour, nursing the same Coke and getting dirty looks from the waitress for taking up space which otherwise could have been occupied by a tipping customer. After another twenty minutes without a sign of a friendly face, I knew I was only moments away from being asked to leave. Rather than face that indignity, I dropped fifteen cents on the counter and headed out the door. I could not for the life of me figure out where everyone could be. There were about six of us who hung together now and again, but Harold Gracie, Donny Lyle, and I were practically inseparable.

Harold was a big, strapping, boisterous guy who had recently arrived from Glace Bay, Nova Scotia, and still had the heavy "down-home" accent to prove it.

Donny was the complete opposite of Harold. He was short and skinny with pale, pock-marked skin. He was a very quiet, unassuming person, and a genuinely nice guy who always seemed to have money. He told me once that his father was a drunk and didn't care much where he went or who he was with any time of the day or night. He didn't abuse Donny; he just ignored him most of the time.

I walked down Carlton toward the Riverdale Zoo hoping to spot Harold or Donny or any of the gang, but by this time it was getting on ten o'clock without the sign of a single friendly face. I had not forgotten about my court-enforced curfew and the likelihood of going back to jail if I was caught out so late. I knew there was only one safe place to go. A place even the cops avoided late at night: Allen Gardens.

The night people of the park tended to be older men who kept to themselves. Most were ragged and dirty, with blackened fingers and the blotchy-skin evidence of exposure to the elements and years of alcohol abuse. They were always wary of strangers, but once they knew you were not a threat they could open up just enough to get a glimpse into their world.

It was far too cool a night to sleep, so I spent most of the early morning hours just moving about trying to stay warm and doing a lot of listening and thinking — and feeling more than a little sorry for myself.

It only took one night to figure out I definitely was not cut out for a life on the street. All anyone had to do was look into the faces of the night people who inhabited the park and see the pain, suffering, and loneliness painted in their eyes. They told me heart-wrenching stories of hunger, families lost from addiction, physical and mental abuse, but most of all they talked of bad choices and missed opportunities from their youth.

Ten o'clock the next morning found me on Yonge Street. After devouring a couple of chocolate bars, I headed for the Rio Theatre were the same three movies played continually all day for 50 cents, and, most important, I could stay warm and dry. At about four in the afternoon I awoke, startled from the noise on the screen. Like the Satellite Restaurant the night before, I knew I best make a move soon before I wore out my welcome. Back on the street I took stock of my situation. I was dirty and hungry and had about six dollars in change left in my pocket. The thoughts of spending another night in the park did not in the least appeal to me.

My brother Michael and his wife Nora lived in a cramped one-bedroom apartment on Eglinton Avenue. I don't think he was too happy with the prospect of having me cluttering up his apartment, but he told me to come over to stay for the night and we could figure something out for the long term. Mike and I didn't have much to do with each other growing up, mainly because he was almost a decade my senior, but I had always felt a special bond toward him. At the age of five I had fallen into the Grand Canal and immediately sank to the deep muddy bottom. Michael didn't hesitate even long enough to take off his shoes before diving straight to the bottom and pulling me safely to shore. The day my mother died it was left to Mike to break the news to all of us younger kids. When I needed someone to get me out of jail, Michael had been the one to show up in the courtroom, and now he would be the one I could rely on to get me off the street.

A week had passed since I had been kicked out of the house. Mike and Nora had taken me in, fed me, and let me sleep on their couch. Their basement apartment was small, with one bedroom, a tiny kitchen, and a living room. Because Mike and Nora worked all day, I would sometimes stand at the front window watching all manner of feet and legs pass me by. Everyone seemed to be in a hurry to get somewhere. They had a purpose to their lives, and I felt myself drifting along without a purpose or plan. It was a depressing time, to say the least.

Michael was not much of a talker. He normally said only what needed saying, except when you got him started on his time in the army. Then his eyes seemed to light up and he could go on and on. He told me of the lifelong friendships he had made and of the good times had while learning to drive the "Deuce and a half" and five-ton trucks. Mike only spent a couple of years in the army before being given a compassionate release after my mother's death in 1962.

All of the talk about the army had convinced me that the military was my best option. The military would get me out of Toronto, but I knew I had to make a radical change if I was ever to show my father that I was not worthless. I wanted desperately to be on my own, out in the world, doing something worthwhile. But most of all I just wanted not to have to rely on anyone — not my friends, not my family, just myself. Only one major hurdle remained: I was just sixteen and would have to wait a few more months until my seventeenth birthday.

During the intervening months I did a succession of meaningless, back-breaking jobs, just to kill time until my birthday. Most of the jobs were strictly bull labour and could have been done by a large, well-trained monkey. The work may have been mind numbingly hard, but there was one hidden benefit. By early October 1964, when I left the job, I was a relatively slim but fit 150 pounds, and I was looking forward to finding what I truly hoped would be a better, more interesting life.

There was one thing left to do before I could apply to the army. I was just seventeen, and to join the forces I would need my father's permission.

As I approached the house and knocked lightly on the front door, I was nervous, to say the least. I had not seen him in over a year. Would he talk to me or even acknowledge my existence? I picked a time when I knew my brothers and sisters were at school and he would be alone in the house. The long walk from the bus stop to the house gave me ample time to practice what I wanted to say. He opened the door almost immediately, and before I could say anything he caught me completely off guard by smiling and inviting me in.

I had not seen him in many months and he looked smaller and thinner than I remembered. It may have been wishful thinking on my part, but his smile and demeanour made me feel that he was genuinely glad to see me. He took only a moment to glance over the consent form before signing it and pushing it back across the table to me. "Do you have time for a cup of tea?" he asked, still smiling.

"No," I said, not knowing why I felt so uncomfortable. "I don't want to hold you up from getting to work and I really have to be somewhere." Less than three minutes later I was well down the road, heading for the bus stop.

Over forty years have passed since that meeting, but rarely a week goes by without thinking about it and regretting not having taken the time to just talk to my Dad that day in the kitchen. I was to see him once more, in 1968, but by then it was too late for talk. He was dying of cancer. He was only conscious for brief periods, but when he spoke there was no recognition in his eyes.

He died in 1969, and every year since then, if I am in the country, I go to his and my mother's grave at Christmas to lay a wreath and spend a little time just talking to him.

It was with more than a little trepidation that I made my way up the subway steps at Yonge and St. Clair looking for the recruiting centre.

Trying to look as confident as possible, I approached the stern-faced sergeant behind the counter and told him I wanted to join. He had the bored look of a man who had asked the same questions about age, height, weight, and education a thousand times. Each of my responses was met by a nod of his head but finally the big question came: citizenship? I hesitated, then mumbled something about not being sure. As I explained about being born in Dublin and immigrating to Canada in 1957, he continually shook his head saying he didn't think I was eligible but to take a seat while he checked.

When he reappeared his negative look had not changed. I came to the counter feeling very deflated and expecting the worst. He examined my Irish birth certificate yet again, and after what seemed an eternity he finally looked up. "Looks like you just made it by just three months."

I was far too relieved to even question it at the time, but found out later that I was deemed to be a British subject because I was born in 1947. Only people born after January 1948 were considered citizens of an independent Ireland.

The very next morning I anxiously sat in the waiting area at Sunnybrook Hospital waiting for my name to be called. I had been warned that the "M Test," as they called it, was a relatively straightforward test of both math and language ability, which was designed to determine what areas of the military best suited an individual's skills.

Immediately after the test I was dispatched to the hospital proper for a medical exam. The doctor asked some questions, checked a number of orifices, and in less than ten minutes pronounced me fit.

By late that afternoon I was back in the waiting room nervously waiting to be called into an office where I was told I would see the PSO (Personnel Selection Officer) and he would tell me the results of my tests and for what trades I was best suited.

I found myself staring at a man sitting directly across from me in battle-dress uniform. Above his breast pocket was a set of parachute wings and below them a row of ribbons. Sewn on his sleeve was a set of cross rifles surmounted by a crown. My curiosity finally got the best of me and I asked what the rifles were for. He answered in one word: "marksmanship." Once he saw I was suitably impressed by this he started to talk. "Which unit was I joining? What trade was I getting?" He looked rather disappointed when I told him I didn't have a clue. He leaned forward, looked left and right and whispered, "Don't let these guys bullshit ya into taking some Mickey Mouse job. Go somewhere you can have fun and see the world!"

He told me he had been an "RCR" for twelve years and had been to Germany, Cyprus, Alaska, and all over the Middle East. As I sat there listening I realized I had no idea that RCR stood for Royal Canadian Regiment, but I was not about to interrupt his fascinating stories by asking a mundane question.

Eventually he sat back and sighed, "Yeah, I was all set to go back to Germany with the battalion next year, but my last parachute jump screwed me up completely and I'm being medically reclassified to another trade." Moments later, my name was called. He winked and wished me luck as I disappeared into the PSO's office.

When I came out some twenty minutes later, he was gone. I often wonder what became of him, and if he knew the effect his words were about to have on my life.

The PSO was the short, thin, and studious-looking type. He continued looking over his glasses at my file as I sat there fidgeting and wondering if he would eventually acknowledge my existence. "Okay," he eventually said, "your test results are not bad. You can go medic or ordnance corps. What will it be?" I understood medic, but ordnance, I had no idea. Not that it mattered, because after my conversation in the waiting room I knew what I wanted. "If it's alright, I would like to go RCR, sir," was all I could manage to get out of my mouth. I may not have known what RCR meant, but they were going to Germany and that sounded just marvellous to this seventeen-year-old mind. He looked surprised for just a moment, but only nodded and started writing something on the bottom of my file. A moment later he looked up, smiling. "You've got it son. Give this to the clerk outside and he will sort you out."

The next two days were a blur of filling in papers, swearing oaths, getting my fingerprints taken, and then finally being handed a train ticket to London, Ontario. On October 31, 1964, I boarded a train at Union Station in Toronto for the two-hour trip to London. It may have been a relatively short distance, but to my mind it was a journey to the start of a very different life and a new beginning.

Chapter 1

Sheep Shit and Cherry Stones

Wolseley Barracks in the 1960s was a lively, dynamic community of about a thousand soldiers, nestled on a relatively small piece of property in the north end of the city of London, Ontario. There were five barrack blocks, the largest of which was the "McKenzie Block," named for the very first recruit to the Royal Canadian Regiment in 1884. The block housed about two hundred soldiers and was to be my home for the next six months of basic training.

As I made my way through the foyer of the block, toward the central staircase, I could not help but notice the high level of activity all around me. There were small knots of soldiers standing around talking, others were sitting in the hall spit-shining their boots. Five or six more were marching up and down the hallways, in their underwear, practicing what looked like drill movements. In the background I could hear the steady twang of some country and western radio station.

On the second floor, the silence was deafening. I could hear the echo of my footsteps on the tile floor as I searched the east wing for my assigned room. Room 247 looked cold, austere, and completely uninviting. There was a metal-frame bed with a small writing desk, a straight-backed chair, and a floor to ceiling wooden locker built into the wall for each of the room's four occupants. The walls were a dull, bluish-grey, and the floor consisted of black and grey linoleum tiles. Had bars been added to the windows, it could have easily passed for a large, albeit exceptionally clean jail, cell.

My meagre belongings took less than five minutes to stow away in the huge wall locker. Judging by the rolled up mattresses and empty lockers, I was the first occupant to arrive. By all appearances it looked like there were only about six or seven people living in our wing of the building.

It was made official the next morning. Our platoon would not start basic training until we had about forty soldiers, and at the rate people were coming in, it would be at least Christmas before we began any formal course. However, as the corporal told us with a sly smile, "I'm sure we can find lots of things to keep you busy."

That same afternoon we were formed up, still in our civvies, and taken to the quartermaster stores to draw equipment and uniforms. Even if we were not soldiers yet, at least we could look the part. The move to the QM stores was our first pitiful attempt at marching as a formed body of troops. I use the word marching lightly, because even with the corporal shouting "Left … Right … Left … Right," over and over again, the seven of us never came close to being in the same step. "Swing your arms, suck in your gut, stick out your chest, and wiggle your bum," he yelled continuously, but to no avail. We prodded on like a bunch of arthritic ducks. When we finally reached the QM, he suddenly yelled, "Halt!" Only the lead man reacted, while the rest of us simply bumped into each other. The corporal just stood there for a moment shaking his head, and I'm sure wondering how he had managed to be stuck with such a bunch of rejects. "Okay girls, just turn toward me and stand still," he said, in his most sarcastic tone.

The days and weeks went by agonizingly slow, with what seemed like endless projects aimed at keeping us busy with every mundane chore imaginable. We washed the hallway floors, then we would wash the walls, and because the dirt, grime, and paint chips would end up running down the tile, we would, once again, wash the same floor. I thought I knew how to make a bed, but it still took many days to master the "army way." It was simple to tell if the bed was wrong, because if you came back from breakfast and everything, including the mattress, was lying in a heap on the floor, it was the corporal's not-so-subtle way of telling you your efforts were unacceptable. It was to be made hospital style, with the top sheet folded over the red blanket. All the edges had to be square, and there could be absolutely no wrinkles. The making of this single, metal frame bed took not less than thirty minutes each morning, with the wrinkle-free look achieved by actually ironing the made bed.

In late December we got the word — we now had a total of forty recruits and formal training could begin in January. The Royal Canadian had existed since 1883, and since that time they had amassed fifty-two battle honours to commemorate actions fought in the northwest Canada rebellion of 1880, the Boer War, both World Wars, and Korea. Hill 70 had been a hard battle fought in the First World War, so henceforth we would be known as Hill 70 Platoon.

Military courses all start the same way, with those in a position of power insisting upon telling us who they were and what was expected of us over the next six months. By the time our coffee break rolled around on that very first training morning we had been spoken to by practically every single authority figure in the unit.

Where we truly lucked out was in our section commander. When Corporal Scotty McBride spoke to us with his slow and concise Scottish accent we listened because we could tell that he knew what he was talking about. He had been there, done it, and if we paid close attention we could do it too. He very rarely shouted, but there was never any doubt when he was upset or angry. There is a saying in the military: "When in danger, when in doubt, run in circles, scream, and shout." Scotty, like most of the good ones, rarely raised his voice. Of all the briefing that first morning, Scotty's took about thirty seconds and definitely made the most sense.

Our section of fourteen recruits stood tentatively at attention, waiting for our section commander to speak. "Right, gentlemen. Whatever it is you need to know about me you will find out in the next few months. What you think you know about yourselves and what you believe you know about the army is probably 100 percent wrong," he said as he continued to pace back and forth in front of us. "You know nothing! Once you realize and accept this fact, we will have a place to start. If you listen to me and work hard learning the skills me and the rest of the staff teach you, six months from now you will have earned the right to be called a soldier. Right now none of you could tell the difference between sheep shit and cherry stones, but by the time we are done I guarantee you will. Questions?" Nobody moved. "Okay." He smiled. "Enough talk. Let's get on with it."

Within a couple of weeks, everything started to develop into a routine. Up at six o'clock, stand in line for a sink, wash and shave in under ten minutes so the next person can get their turn. Then it was back to the room for twenty minutes of bed making. Another twenty minutes or so of dusting, polishing, and laying out on the bed whatever was being inspected that morning. All this time we stayed in our underwear so as not to in any way stain or wrinkle the uniform.

Last came the most intricate operation: getting dressed. In the beginning this could take upwards of forty-five minutes, with most of the time spent getting the bootlaces tight and flat, followed by snapping on the lead weights around each leg. After this it was a matter of slowly and precisely rolling on the putties so that each of the required three rolls was evenly spaced an inch apart starting at the third eyelet from the top and ending eight inches up the shin. Once the putties were in place, it was a simple matter of moving the weights down to create an evenly bloused effect around the bottom of the battle dress trousers.

With the boots laced snugly on our feet and the putties wrapped tight enough to impede circulation, coupled with the two lead weights dangling at the bottom of the trousers, I was always amazed that none of us developed varicose veins from our knees to our necks. Once the tunic was buttoned up, all that remained was the web belt with the brass regimental buckle, which we were always careful not to touch with our bare, greasy hands. After spending a lot of time the night before applying Brasso and rubbing it until it glistened, the last thing we needed was a fingerprint or smudge.

The level of activity in preparation for morning inspection depended mainly upon what day of the week it was. Monday and Tuesday we generally had our section corporal come through. Scotty McBride was extremely thorough, rarely missing any fault in either your kit layout or uniform. The mid-week inspections by the sergeant major were the most intense and nerve-wracking of all. By the time he finished our room would be littered with over-turned beds and all manner of kit and equipment he found to be sub-standard.

The moment the morning inspection began the mad scramble to get our kit secured in the locker because we all knew what was coming next. "You have exactly thirty seconds to get outside," the marching NCO yelled. "Move! Move! Move!" Being last to fall in assured you of being on the duty corporal's inspection that night. The sound of forty sets of hobnailed boots thundering down the stairs reminded me of the running of the bulls at Pamplona. We were like wild animals in a panic, all pushing and shoving not to be last.

During those first few weeks of training we always seemed to be moving at breakneck speed. Out of the quarters, fall in, and march to the lecture training building for lessons on everything from the rifle, first aid, military history, and even personal hygiene.

The hygiene lectures always seemed to centre around social diseases and the dire consequences should you be unfortunate enough to get either gonorrhea or syphilis. The old Second World War black and white films we watched on this subject were guaranteed to frighten any seventeen year old out of the thought of ever having sex.

After an hour or two in a stuffy lecture room, we were off to the parade square for some much needed drill. Once the NCOs started yelling words of command and the February winds started to blow, the exhilaration of being outside quickly wore off.

The physical training (PT) classes alternated between a combination of running and floor exercises and the most dreaded periods of all: swimming. Although the running shoes for PT may have been simple canvas sneakers with absolutely no arch support, at least we had something on our feet. For swim classes we had nothing. I don't believe they ever fully explained why we had to swim naked.

A more pathetic sight you could not imagine. Fifty naked, scrawny, and shivering men, all standing there trying desperately not to look too self-conscious while the cold water and drafty surroundings all conspired to shrink and shrivel our privates. Finally, the instructor would arrive and tell us to take a seat around the edge of the pool, while he explained what lesson we would cover that day. The sound of fifty naked bums hitting the tile always sounded to me like a short round of applause.

After eight weeks of being locked away on the base we were about to be given the opportunity to gain some limited amount of freedom. The last hurdle to cross before we could walk out the front gate was to pass the saluting test.

When the big day came we all waited nervously in the drill hall for the regimental sergeant major (RSM) to arrive. The RSM would stand off to the side and observe as each person's name was called. All of us were anxiously awaiting his arrival and going over and over in our minds exactly what had to be done. As my name was called, I yelled, "Sir," and marched down the drill hall floor past the first marker where I saluted to the right. I continued to march forward to a position directly in front of the next marker where I halted and saluted, followed by a pause, after which I turned about and marched back down the floor. The marker I passed on the way up was now saluted as I went by it on the left. Once back in my original position, I waited with a great deal of anticipation for the RSM pass or fail decision.

After a moment of thought for each performance, the RSM would decide our fate by a simple head movement. If he nodded yes, the platoon sergeant placed a check mark next to the name on his list, meaning that person had passed. However, if the RSM shook his head, the X on the paper denoted a failure. A failure meant we could look forward to two more weeks of being confined to the base before attempting the test again.

Those of us who passed would be allowed to leave the confines of Wolseley Barracks, as long as we were back in the quarters by ten o'clock each night.

More important than simply being allowed out, the saluting test also meant we had reached our first significant milestone. The first phase of training, with all of those endless classroom lessons, was complete and we could shift our focus to working in the field.

Until then, much of what we had learned had been theory, but now we would start to learn the practical application of how to live and fight in the field. The first step toward this was mastering the use of the FN C1 Rifle, and to achieve this we were about to spend the first of many weeks on the range.

It is difficult to find a more desolate place in the dead of winter than the Cedar Springs Rifle Range. Butting up against Lake Erie and about an hour's drive west of London, it had little or nothing to offer, other than a six-hundred-yard range and a constant cold wind whipping steadily off the lake. At the back of the range there were a number of old, drafty buildings. Their peeling paint and generally weather-beaten appearance were testament to the ever erosive winds blowing off the lake to the south. The largest of the buildings served as our recruit quarters. It was a long, narrow affair, with double bunks down each side and a large, pot-bellied stove in the middle of the floor, which was the only source of heat. It didn't take long to realize that to stay warm one needed to be within twenty feet of the stove. Outside that distance the temperature dropped dramatically.

The rifle range itself was a simple affair. It was six hundred yards long, with raised firing mounds every one hundred yards. A thirty-foot man-made hill, called a bullet stop, ran the width of the range, and as one can guess from the name, its purpose was to stop any bullets going beyond the range and into Lake Erie.

All things considered, our first week in Cedar Springs had been a productive one. Some had done very well firing the rifle, while others, like me, had managed to scrape through with a pass. I knew I would never be on the rifle team, but regardless of this I felt content in the knowledge that I could do it, and with more time and experience I could only get better.

March turned to April and brought with it mild temperatures, which turned the training area into a wet, muddy mess. The rising morning temperature would turn the dirt tracks to porridge, which would quickly turn to deep frozen ruts once the sun went down in late afternoon.

We were about to enter the third and last phase of recruit training, with the vast majority of our time spent in the field, learning tactics.

Camp Ipperwash was a beautiful little training area situated on Lake Huron, just west of the town of Grand Bend. The base itself consisted of long *H*-shaped buildings, similar to those found at Cedar Springs, only here they appeared to be in pristine condition and there were a great deal more of them.

Although the quarters were rather austere, at least they were warm. We only spent a couple of days inside, and then moved out to the training area proper for our first taste of battle tactics and survival training.

The morning fog and frost haze had barely lifted each morning when we would be bouncing along the dirt road leading to the ranges. The combination of heavy trucks and slush turned the dirt track into a muddy slippery mess, with icy-water-filled potholes every few yards. The old 1951 pattern truck, otherwise known as the "Deuce and a Half," would just grind along in low gear, with twenty of us recruits hanging on for dear life in the back. We knew when we were approaching another pothole because the driver would gun the engine and attack the obstacle, never letting up on the gas for fear of sinking up to the axle in mud. "Hang on!" he would scream. We in the back would brace ourselves on the wooden bench seat, knowing full well that every bone in our bodies was about to be rattled. As the wheel of the truck found the bottom of the hole, the entire chassis would suddenly drop, with gravity forcing our bodies straight up for just a split second, followed by the violent downwards crashing of your butt against the bench, while simultaneously the lower back and spine slammed into the metal superstructure.

Thus far our weapons skills were restricted to the rifle, submachine gun, and pistol, but now we were getting into the more formidable weapons — starting with grenades.

There is no feeling quite like holding a live grenade in your hand for the first time, knowing that once you pull that pin and release the striker lever you have about six seconds before it explodes. Naturally it was with a bit of nervousness and a lot of anticipation that we moved through the steps leading up to the actual throwing.

A grenade range is rather a simple affair, with a thirty-foot tower in the centre and a throwing bay of reinforced concrete on either side. Once the command to throw is given, you simply remove the safety pin, draw the right arm back, and throw the grenade like you would a baseball. Naturally, normal instinct tells you to immediately duck down and take cover behind the wall, but we were expected to do just the opposite. The corporal tells you to remain standing to see exactly where the thing lands, so that if it doesn't go off you will know precisely where it is when you go out to find it. Once the grenade strikes the ground and stops rolling, then and only then can you take cover. It is amazing how long six seconds is when you are watching the flight of a grenade through the air.

It had taken over three months on rather dull classroom lessons, but by the end of day two in Ipperwash, we finally fired all of the weapons used in an infantry platoon. Putting a 250 belt of ammunition through a .30-calibre machinegun is, without doubt, an exhilarating experience.

Having successfully fired the machinegun and thrown grenades we were all just a little cocky and feeling our confidence level continually increase. The last thing to fire before we moved on to field tactics was the rocket launcher, and we all looked forward to this with eager anticipation. Unfortunately, the 3.5-inch rocket launcher was a notoriously unreliable piece of kit that more often than not misfired, especially in cold weather. That day was no exception. I had the distinction of being the first firer, with my roommate, Frank Whalen, acting as my loader.

As soon as Frank yelled "Ready," I set the safety lever to fire, bent my knees, and leaned forward, knowing that once I hit the trigger the missile would ignite and explode down the tube with tremendous force. The trick was to hold it as steady as possible and not flinch through the noisy and powerful detonation phase. I tried to relax my breathing while slowly and precisely placing the cross-hairs of the sight on the tank target some two hundred yards ahead. *Steady, relax,* I reminded myself as I took careful aim and applied pressure to the trigger.

The silence was deafening. One, two, then ten seconds went by before I realized that nothing had happened. "Damn it!" is all I could think to say. I continued to hold the loaded weapon on my shoulder, never taking my eye off the target. *Okay, Burke. Remember your misfire drill,* I muttered to myself. "Misfire!" I screamed out as I instinctively re-cocked the weapon. Again I applied pressure to the trigger, only this time my breathing was becoming a bit laboured as I tried to steady the crosshairs on the centre of the target. It had been well over a minute since I took up the aim and my focus was becoming a little blurred, but still I vainly attempted to hold it on as I squeezed the trigger.

The sudden explosion as the missile rocketed out of the tube caught me by surprise as the launcher jumped upwards off my shoulder. I had hardly regained control before I saw the missile arc toward the target and detonate its high explosive warhead against the turret ring, scant inches above where I had been aiming.

By late afternoon we finally had the last of the rockets fired and we were all looking forward to getting back to the shack for a warm up and one last good night's sleep before we moved out to the field for our final exercise in tactics and survival training. That's when we were hit with a little surprise. "All right, ladies.

As you have no doubt noticed by now the trucks are not here," he paused for effect. "That's because we won't need them," again he paused, only this time a big grin started to fill his face. "The exercise starts now, and we're going to walk to the area! Right, pick up your kit, turn to your left, quick march!"

By nightfall we had marched and stumbled some three miles across open fields and through the underbrush. The only noise heard in the dark was the rattling of loose equipment, the heavy breathing of this forced exertion, and the odd curse as someone stepped into semi-frozen, water-filled hole or stumbled over the numerous tank ruts in our path. Suddenly we were given the word to halt as the dark silhouette of our deuce and a half truck rolled out of the woods before us. "Okay, ladies. We have not got all night. Move to the truck, get your rucksacks, and start building a shelter for the night."

Had this been the real thing and the enemy was over ten miles away, he still would have had no difficulty hearing us as we blindly stumbled about in the dark, trying to build some kind of shelter from the elements. Someone had lit a match, which resulted in an instant scream from one of the NCOs to get rid of it before he came over and shoved it up the culprit's ass. Another hour of stumbling and grumbling and slowly the noise went away, only to be replaced by the snoring of exhausted soldiers.

It seemed we had only just closed our eyes when the platoon sergeant came tearing through the position, kicking sleeping bags, while banging mess tins together and bellowing commands. "Okay, ladies. Drop your cocks and grab your socks. Let's go, let's go," he repeated. "Daylight is burning and you people are wasting the best part of the day!" The dampness coming out of the frozen ground and the body sweat from the lack of air circulation inside the sleeping bag combined to produce a mind- and bone-chilling numbness. Everywhere you looked people were jumping about, flailing their arms and running on the spot, all in a vain effort to try getting some warmth back into their bodies.

By eight o'clock the sun had finally peeked over the horizon and some feeling began to return to our shivering bodies. We all began to look forward to the appearance of the quartermaster with breakfast and, most importantly, hot coffee. We had finally managed to pack up all our kit and were ready to move, but still there was no sign of food or drink. The order to get our gear on and fall into line came with the usual shouts to hurry it up coming from the NCOs. Just as we were about to step off, the platoon sergeant stopped in mid sentence, "Oh, I almost forgot. To save the tax payers some money, I have decided that you could all go without breakfast this morning. Besides, after your piss poor performance last night none of you deserve the right to government rations!"

By mid-morning we were charging about the sand dunes at the extreme northern edge of the Ipperwash training area. At least the physical activity was keeping us warm and our minds off our empty stomachs. Even with the hunger, damp clothes, and the uncomfortable feeling of sand invading every bodily crevice, the chance to run through mock attacks with blank ammunition firing and the explosion of gunpowder charges going off was truly exhilarating. By the time lunch arrived we were well warmed up, tired, filthy dirty, and starving, but despite it all we were a happy, boisterous group.

It had been a hard six months and we had lost a few people along the way. Forty frightened faces had peered up to the dais at the front of the classroom that first morning listening as one after another our officers and NCOs told us how things would be. Some had been lost to illness or broken bones, some had failed and been sent back to redo the training with later recruit platoons, and still others had simply folded under the pressure and gone "absent without leave." Now less than twenty-five members of Hill 70 Platoon remained to march onto the parade square for our final time as recruits.

Hill 70 Platoon graduation day, May 1965. In the front row, Joy Payton is second from the left and Scotty McBride is seated third from right. In the middle row, I can be seen second from the left, and second from the right is Bob Stuckless.

• • •

Any idea we may have had about life in the battalion being easier was quickly dispelled. After only a couple of days of inactivity we awoke to the sound of loud screaming and garbage can lids being banged together like cymbals. "Get your lazy asses out into the hallway, now!" the voice insisted.

Tommy Stoke was to be our first platoon sergeant in the battalion, and a scarier man I was yet to meet. He probably topped out at five foot ten inches and 160 pounds, but even through the heavy battle dress uniform you could tell there was little other than solid muscle to this man.

There was a deafening silence as he waited for each man to fall in. When the last person got into position, Sergeant Stoke finally spoke. This time his voice was low and restrained, but we could tell from the tone that this was no man to trifle with.

"As you will see over these next few weeks and months I am probably one of the most even tempered NCOs you are even likely to meet. However, when I give an order I expect you to react immediately." He continued, with his voice slowly rising, "What I need from you … No. What I *demand* from all of you is your undivided attention, so that when you are given an order you carry it out quickly, correctly, and without question. If I say jump, you say how high. If I say shit, you say how much. You are not here to discuss decisions; this is not a democracy. You may at some point in your career go to some foreign country to help restore democracy, but let there be no doubt in your military mind, our job is to defend democracy, not to practice it!"

By early June of 1965 our lives had become a series of boring routines, punctuated by the rare bit of exciting training. We thought we knew all that was necessary to be a good soldier, but each day we learned something new.

Morning was usually spent in the classroom on subjects varying from first aid to CPR, unarmed combat and bayonet fighting. I always found it ironic that not only were we learning to fight with and without weapons, but if we did manage to get injured or stabbed, at least we would know how to stop the bleeding. The afternoons we spent in the sports field or gym, putting whatever theory we had learned into practical use.

Although all of this training was designed to give us a broader under-standing of the soldiering trade, none of it covered more than a very basic knowledge on the subjects. What we all needed and hoped for was some specialty training, not only so we could get a more in-depth knowledge and experience on weaponry, but, more important, with a specialty qualification came increased status and pay. With the successful completion of a weapons course came an extra $12 a month, plus our official military status went from being "Private Recruit" to "Private Trained."

At last the course list we had all been anxiously waiting for was published. For me it was to be the anti-tank course which was scheduled to start in just three days and take approximately five weeks to complete.

The 106 mm recoilless rifle was the big gun, in both the physical and literal sense. A well-trained crew could engage and destroy any main battle tank, whether stationary or moving, out to distances of about 1,500 yards. The gun was about twelve feet long from muzzle to breech.

We had gone through hundreds of dry drills during the theory portion of the course, but there is nothing that can really prepare you for kneeling with your face just inches away from a gun breech when it fires a missile out the front and spits a 150-foot flame out the back. In that split second of detonation, the force of the blow draws the skin on your neck and face taut while all the air in your lungs is sucked from your body. Next comes a moment of searing heat, as the blast of flames and smoke snaps your head back. To make the whole experience just a bit worse, we had absolutely no hearing protection. As ludicrous as it may sound today, the belief back then was that a person putting plugs or cotton or any type of protective device in their ears could not properly hear the commands given on the gun line and was therefore unsafe.

As luck would have it, when the last day of firing rolled around, the week of steady rain finally let up. The sun peeked through by early afternoon as we hurried to finish cleaning and oiling up the guns in preparation for our return to London. Despite the skin-deep dampness we felt from our wet clothes, and the continuing buzzing in our ears, we were a very happy group. We were finally qualified as "Trained Soldiers."

Although this was my first weapons specialty qualification, by the time we departed for London I had already made up my mind that doing this full time, as a member of anti-tank platoon, was not something I wanted to do.

The night before we left for home was our one and only free evening of the week. After supper I made my way over to the wet canteen, in the hope of perhaps having a beer or two.

Six or seven of us had managed to crowd around one of the few empty tables. Three of us were from the anti-tank course, two others were just finishing the mortar course, but all the conversation was directed toward the last man in our little group, who had just finished the assault pioneer course.

Unlike the majority of weapons specialties, to master the assault pioneer course you had to successfully complete tests in explosives, mine warfare, watermanship, bridging, field fortifications, and field geometry. Of the original twenty six candidates just eighteen had passed, but only five had achieved high enough marks to actually make it into the platoon.

I knew what I wanted to do and where I wanted to be, but I was smart enough to know just how daunting a task I faced. Being selected for the course and then actually passing was difficult enough. Even if I successfully achieved both of these aims, I still faced the extremely tough task of actually getting into pioneer platoon.

Summer finally arrived, and the battalion went into high gear in preparations for rotation to Germany. By then our platoon had expanded to include two more corporals and one new second lieutenant.

Our new section commander, Corporal Reg Evers, was a big man. With his stubby, blond, brush-cut hair, deep set eyes, and ruddy complexion, set atop a 220 pound, six-foot frame, he was the very definition of everything we thought a soldier should be, or at least look like.

As we found out later, he and Sergeant Stoke were old friends from pioneer platoon and now Corporal Evers had been temporarily assigned to our company to assist in preparing us for the impending move to Germany.

Not long after he arrived in Bravo Company, he and I had our first of many encounters as he stopped me just inside the entrance to the quarters. "What's your name, boy?" As he spoke his index finger continued to poke solidly into my chest. Each thrust inched me back until I was firmly pinned against the corridor wall.

"I'm Burke, Private Burke," I stuttered loudly.

"Well Burke, Private Burke, have you ever been on TV?" Having no idea what he was talking about, I just stared blankly ahead. "You're not that rodeo rider Stoney Burke that used to be on television?" I thought this man was obviously insane, but all I could manage to do was mumble and shake my head. "Well, Stoney," he went on with his questions, "I understand you are interested in being a pioneer?" I nodded my head, but just as I started to speak he cut me off. "I'm not so sure a young snot like you has what it takes, but we'll have to wait and see." I had no real idea what he meant, but before I could say anything, he walked away.

He never brought it up again, but after he referred to me a few times by my new nickname, the handle soon stuck. In my years in the military I must have known hundreds, if not thousands, of soldiers, most of whom never knew my real name. It became Stoney that day, and so it would remain for over forty years.

By late August, the activity surrounding the imminent rotation of the entire battalion to Germany was reaching a fevered pitch. One hundred and one details on each person had to be checked and then checked again. The paperwork alone was daunting.

There was one critical step in the clearance procedure to which none of us were looking forward. When Corporal Evers told us to fall in that morning, wearing only our t-shirts, we knew it could only mean one thing: needles parade.

As we entered the drill hall, the medics were lined up about three feet apart and facing each other. Rather than a single hypodermic, each one held a needle gun, capable of firing a shot of serum into our waiting arms. Our job was to walk through the gauntlet of needles, with both arms extended. The trick was to keep moving slowly forward, always looking straight ahead, as each medic, in turn, stuck his gun against your outstretched arm and fired. The medical officer sat near the end of the gauntlet looking rather bored. His job was to tend to the one in ten to fifteen soldiers who keeled over in a dead faint on the cement floor. Whether the fainting was caused by a bad reaction to the serum injection or simply a case of nerves, the patient usually recovered quickly. However, the bumps and bruises from hitting the drill hall floor normally took a good deal longer to go away. Strangely enough, whenever a soldier "kissed the cement," those of us who had managed to make it through would immediately start laughing and jeering at the poor sot, while those still waiting to enter the gauntlet stayed nervously silent.

By early autumn, the long days and nights of training were finally drawing to a close. I was surprised to learn that I was to be on the advance party departing for Germany in early October 1965.

When Sergeant Stoke had called me into his office to give me the news, he greeted me at the door with a huge, toothy smile. Ever since he had gotten the word that he was taking over as the pioneer platoon sergeant his attitude toward us had been downright mellow. I knew this was my opportunity to speak to him about something which had been percolating in my mind ever since I had been at gun camp months earlier. "Sergeant Stoke," I began tentatively. "I was wondering if you could tell me when the next pioneer course is running and if perhaps you could help me get on it?" I think my request caught him a little off guard, but he quickly recovered.

"We usually don't take such junior soldiers, but I'll see what I can do." It wasn't the response I was hoping for, but I thanked him and started to leave. Seeing the dejected look on my face, he stopped me at the door. "Tell you what, Burke. If you are truly interested, see me when we get to Germany and I'll give you some of the course material you can study in your spare time. We won't be running a course until at least January, but if can show me you are willing to study and make the effort, I'll see what I can do."

The hostility of Corporal Evers when I ran into him the next morning was rather perplexing. Since our first encounter weeks earlier, the subject of me going to pioneers had never come up, until now. Gone was his usual friendly greeting. "Well, Burke, what makes you think a rookie like you can make it in pioneers?" Before I could answer, he continued his disparaging remarks. "Sergeant Stoke may like you, but I'll be the lead instructor on the course, and I'm the one you'll have to impress." As usual, his negative comments were followed by an abrupt departure. His harsh comments did little to dampen my enthusiasm.

Although the aircraft would not depart Trenton until sometime past seven o'clock that evening, I was already sitting on my barrack box, in the corner of the drill hall, at nine o'clock in the morning, anxiously awaiting the arrival of the bus. The hall was crowded with women and children, all there to say goodbye to their departing husbands. Some of the more senior members of the unit had their families on the aircraft, but the vast majority of women and children would have to wait for their husbands to get to Germany and find a place to live. I sat there feeling quite self-conscious as husbands held hands and whispered consoling words to their wives. Children wrapped their arms around daddy's legs crying, not knowing what was going on. I tried not to intrude on these private moments by keeping my face buried in some pocket novel, pretending to read.

By early afternoon, we were well on our way down Highway 401. The unusually warm, sunny morning had given way to a slow, steady drizzle as we moved passed the city of Toronto.

I sat there staring out, trying to discern familiar streets and buildings through the ripples of rain flowing sideways down the window. Passing by the open fields near Dufferin Street, I could just make out the roofs of houses, very close to where we had lived in North York. As we passed the Yonge Street exit

I thought about my mother buried just to the north, in Holy Cross Cemetery. Crossing over the Don Valley, I couldn't help but remember those many long ago summer afternoons sitting on the banks of the Don River fishing for suckers.

I was not unhappy to finally get past the city and all things familiar. I looked at my watch and smiled, thinking we were making good time. Soon this first part of the trip would be over, but the next part of the journey would cover thousands of miles and take the better part of five years to complete.

Chapter 2
House Mouse or Shack Rat

The high pitch of the propellers made all normal conversation impossible, even with the person sitting next to you. The noise was accompanied by a steady, unrelenting vibration throughout the aircraft. When the cabin staff served a meal, it had to be eaten with one hand, while the other held the tray and its contents in place.

After eleven hours of unrelenting noise and vibration, it felt absolutely marvelous to finally step off the four engine Yukon Aircraft and to once again feel the solid, unmoving ground beneath my feet. We were finally in Germany. All that remained was a two hour bus ride to our home in Fort York.

The five thousand man Canadian Mechanized Brigade Group made up a small component of the British Army on the Rhine (BAOR). The BAOR was certainly a formidable fighting force of British and Canadians, but it was only part of a much larger NATO force of Americans, Belgians, Dutch, and French stretching from Norway to the Swiss Border. Despite the tens of thousands of soldiers deployed to protect NATOs northern flank, it was nothing compared to the hundreds of thousands of Warsaw Pact soldiers the experts assumed were just sitting and waiting to pour out of the east and steamroll straight through Western Europe, all the way to the French coast.

In this the third decade of the Cold War, most believed that the question wasn't if they would come, but only when it was going to happen.

Although we had been given many briefings on the military situation before leaving Canada, it had all seemed rather surreal. Now it was different. With the East German border roughly sixty-two miles away, it didn't take a military expert to realize we were sitting right in the middle of what could be ground zero for the Third World War. Although this was rather heady stuff for someone who had just passed his eighteenth birthday, it was nonetheless something kept in the dark recesses of the mind, but never too far from the surface.

An aerial view of Fort York Germany, circa 1965.

A rainy day inspection on the parade square in Fort York.

As we approached the camp, it took a few minutes to realize that Fort York was in fact a military base. Even the high chain-link fence surrounding the encampment was partially obscured by large pine trees and bushy undergrowth.

If I had to sum up my initial impression of the base in one word, it would be "inconspicuous." Of the seventy-five or so buildings that made up the camp, none were more than one storey high. Fort York, along with the other six Canadian bases, sat smack in the middle of the Ruhr Valley, in the industrialized heart of Northern Germany.

A series of low, narrow, whitewashed buildings surrounded three sides of the massive parade square. Each building housed about eighty soldiers, arranged in four separate wings. The quarters were dissected through the middle by a common area of showers, toilets, and sinks. It was an austere setting to say the least, with each person having only enough room for a narrow metal-frame bed, a locker, and a small bedside table. Those fortunate enough to live on the outer walls at least had the luxury of opening a window to combat the odours which inevitably accompany eighty men living in close proximity to each other. Those relegated to the inside wall had nothing but the metal furniture, cinderblock walls, and a cement floor to call home.

With so little personal space, each person's tiny domain was fiercely guarded. Entering another soldier's area uninvited often resulted in angry words being exchanged, and for those who failed to heed the initial warning, a full-blown fist fight usually followed.

Security of personal kit was also among our major concerns. With so many people living in each building there was a constant flow of foot traffic through the open corridor of each wing. To leave money or a wallet sitting on a bedside table, even when you went for a shower, was asking for trouble. Unlike our penniless existence back in Canada, now we had a good deal more money. Soldiers serving outside of Canada received an additional hundred dollars in what was called "Foreign Service Allowance," which increased our overall pay to a whopping $200 per month.

I had been in Germany for just one week when I got my first object lesson on security, albeit at the expense of someone else. I had some letters to write one evening and had gone to supper early with the idea of getting back to the peace and quiet of the shack while most people were still eating. My high hopes were quickly dashed when I walked through the door, only to find Teddy Howard wandering around, muttering to himself. It took just a moment to realize that Teddy was more than a little agitated. Realizing that I was not the target of his anger, I tried calming him down. "Relax, Ted. Just tell me what happened." He finally took a deep breath, went over to his side table, lit a cigarette, and threw the lighter onto his bed in disgust.

"I got back from house hunting about three o'clock and thought I'd take a quick nap before supper. While I was asleep some bastard took the two twenty mark bills I had lying there next to my wallet!" I thought about suggesting he go to the military police, but we both knew it would do no good. The first question they would ask was whether the money was secure, and when he told them the circumstances they would simply shrug their shoulders and tell him it was his own fault.

Then the strangest thing happened. Ted looked at me and started to smile. "I got an idea on how to catch this bastard," he announced, still smiling. I listened intently as he laid out his plan. It was a rather simple-minded idea, I thought, but possibly just dumb enough to work. The trap would be sprung the following evening.

As Yogi Berra used to say, "It was like déjà vu all over again." When I returned from supper the next evening, Ted was once again walking up and down the floor, cursing and swearing, and kicking beds and lockers. I knew it was a safe assumption that his plan had not worked, but as he explained what had happened, I found it extremely difficult to try and at least look sympathetic, when all I really wanted to do was burst out laughing.

He had purposely gotten back to the quarters early that afternoon and laid his wallet, watch, and money on the bedside table, being careful to make sure there were two loose twenty mark bills sitting invitingly on top for all to see. He then curled up on his bed, closed his eyes in a fake sleep, and waited for the rat to enter his trap. "I heard lots of people come and go, but after another half hour, still no bites." His voice started to rise again as he became visibly angry. "I don't know what happened," he said, pounding his fist against the locker. "I guess with all the waiting, I must have dozed off for a few minutes? When I woke up and realized what happened, I jumped up, but my money was gone! Can you fuckin' believe it?"

• • •

While the eight hundred soldiers of the departing battalion were busy clearing out of the base, we began the daunting process of taking over all the bits and pieces necessary to getting a fully mechanized battalion up and running.

From the commanding officer down to the lowliest private soldier, everyone had something to do and precious little time to get it done. Every vehicle, tool, radio, and weapon had to be checked and counted. Even the furniture in all the buildings had to be accounted for and ready to be turned over to the new battalion in less than forty days. Aside from all of this, the married soldiers had to find some place for their family to live. There was a limited amount of married quarters some six miles away in the city of Soest, but the majority of soldiers would have to go "house hunting" on the German economy to find something suitable.

We had been standing outside the quarters for about twenty minutes that first morning, all still a little overtired from the trip and time change. At last the company sergeant major arrived and briefed us on what was to be the routine for the next few weeks. There had been about 110 people on the aircraft, but once the senior officers and dependents wives and children had gone their separate ways the evening before, we were left with about fifty soldiers ready to start work that first morning.

The sergeant major's first announcement caught me by surprise. "Hands up those who are single," he said, scanning the group. Although none of the guys I had done recruit training with had come over yet, I assumed that at least a few of the soldiers on our aircraft were single. I quickly realized my assumption had been incorrect, when I looked around and saw that I was the lone person with his hand in the air. Even the sergeant major looked a little surprised as he told me to report to him right after lunch when he would brief me on my duties.

The formal name for the job is "Barrack Warden," but most of the guys referred to it as "Shack Rat," "House Mouse," or, most descriptive of all, "Hut Slut." Regardless of the label you put on it, the job was the same. I was to spend each day washing sinks and toilets, mopping floors, and doing whatever other menial cleaning job was necessary in our quarters.

Days turned into weeks, and the numbers grew slowly as more and more flights arrived. By the start of the third week, most of the married guys had managed to secure accommodation for their families, so each day the numbers of empty bed spaces in the shack increased. The few that still remained in quarters looked more and more disheartened as they returned each evening without finding a suitable place to live. I did notice that a small number of them were getting back to the shack later and later each evening, and judging by their staggered walk and boozy breath, it did not appear that a lot of effort had gone into house hunting.

It was about one in the morning when our entire wing was awakened by the sound of slamming doors and the overhead lights being flicked on. Hank Hamer was more than a little intoxicated. He staggered down the floor, slowly trying to make his way to his bed, while talking to himself, ricocheting off lockers, and bumping into tables. Each collision was met with threats from some and laughter from others.

At last Hank managed to navigate his way into his bed space, but the noise was far from over. Someone had jumped up and turned out the overhead light, leaving Hank to stumble around, trying in vain to find his bedside lamp. If anyone had managed to stay asleep up to this point, that was about to change. Hank at last found the lamp, but lost his balance as he reached to turn it on. The lamp and table, along with Hank, all toppled over and crashed to the floor.

Our anger soon turned to laughter when we turned on the light and saw Hank just lying there, on the floor, in a dejected heap. After being helped onto his bed, we once again switched off the lights and tried to get back to sleep.

I had burrowed my way deep down under the blankets in an effort to get back to sleep quickly, and was just milliseconds away from achieving my aim when I heard the distinct sound of crying and moaning coming from Hank's bed space. Slowly the sound increased as Hank mumbled to himself. "What the fuck am I going to do?" He moaned. "I am a useless waste of oxygen and don't deserve to live."

Finally, one of the guys hearing all this, jumped out of bed, flung open his locker, grabbed a tie and threw it at Hank. "There you go Hamer," he said in frustration. "You wanna die, use this to hang yourself! But do it quietly, in the bathroom, so the rest of us can get some sleep!"

Hank bolted off the bed with some newfound coordination and, grabbing the tie, headed toward the bathroom. "I'll show you fuckers!" he said, storming down the hall and into the shower room. Just a few moments had gone by before we all could hear the sound of the heavy shower bench being dragged across the floor. Another second or two of silence passed, and we strained to hear what was going on. No one was sleeping, and you could feel the anticipation as we all sat waiting in our bed, undecided on what to do next. In less than a minute, the sound of crashing and banging made the decision for us.

We all went thundering into the shower room and were met by a sight that was both comical and sad.

Hank had pulled the heavy bench sideways across the floor, to a position directly under the front of one of the shower stalls. He had knotted the tie around his neck, and then, standing on the bench, he had tied the other end securely to the shower curtain rod. Once all was in place, he had jumped off the bench, assuming that the drop, along with the force of the sudden extra weight, would tighten the knot around his neck and death would follow quickly.

His plan was foolproof, right up to the point where he jumped off the bench. The sudden addition of his weight caused the flimsy curtain bar to dislodge from its bracket, striking Hank in the head at just about the same moment that he crashed down on the shower room floor.

We all stood there, trying not to laugh at the pathetic sight of Hank lying in a heap, with the plastic curtain, shower rod, and tie all still firmly suspended around his neck. All he had to show for his efforts was a large red bruise on his forehead where the bar had struck him. "I am one sorry son of a bitch. I can't even kill myself properly." He continued to moan and cry as we helped him up and carried him to his bed. Within five minutes the sound of his snoring told me that the incident was over.

The following afternoon at lunch I saw Hank for the first time since the incident. Other than a swollen forehead and a hangover, he seemed his normal self. I had quickly repaired the minor damage to the shower room stall earlier that morning, not wanting the sergeant major to see it and ask unwanted questions. Before leaving the shack for his house hunting that afternoon, Hank stopped by my bed space and rather sheepishly thanked me for cleaning up the mess he had made. "Today," he said, "I'll find a place come hell or high water!"

It actually took two days, but a couple of weeks later when I saw him packing up his kit and going to the airport to meet his family, he looked like a different man, with a new sense of purpose. "Hanging Hank" was gone for good.

• • •

Those first few weeks in Germany had kept me quite busy. As the barracks emptied out, the job of Hut Slut became far less time consuming. By the time the sergeant major came through for his eleven o'clock inspection, the place was sparkling. Afternoons were spent reading through the stack of books and pamphlets given to me by Sergeant Stoke. I may not have understood much of the material, but fortunately there was always a couple of the older pioneer soldiers around to answer my many questions.

The days were fine, but I dreaded the long lonely evenings when I had little to do and few friends to talk to. The guys in the shack were friendly enough but the majority were older, married soldiers whom I had very little in common with and who generally treated me as the know-nothing kid.

On one occasion, shortly after we had arrived, I decided to venture into the canteen and sample my first German beer. At least here there was no canteen corporal and no one seemed to worry about a legal drinking age. The canteen consisted of just one large room, with a number of six-foot-long tables scattered haphazardly about, and surrounded by gaudy, orange plastic chairs. All four walls were of a pasty yellow colour, with not so much as a single picture or plaque to break the monotony. The dark linoleum floor only added to the inhospitable atmosphere of the place. The serving bar seemed almost like an after-thought, with its cheap vinyl front and laminated top protruding out from one of the side walls. *No wonder all the younger soldiers spent their free time downtown drinking*, I thought. Beer in the canteen may be half the price, but it had all the ambience of a funeral parlour.

Hidden at the back of the room was the single piece of furniture which stood out from all the rest. It was a large, round, wooden table with ornately decorated legs. Eight leather-backed chairs surrounded the table. This small, secluded area looked completely at odds with the rest of the cheap, plain furniture that filled the room.

At the moment, there were about fifteen people scattered about the room, with the majority grouped together at the tables closest to the bar and four more in the opposite corner playing darts. Although I knew most of the customers by sight, I knew none of them well enough to sit and converse with. The big wooden table at the back of the room had four older guys grouped around it, all obviously drunk and talking loudly.

The German lady serving behind the bar gave me a friendly smile as she expertly poured a beer into a long slender glass, making sure that the foamy head rose high above the top, without even a single drop escaping down the side of the glass. My curiosity got the best of me, so I asked her what the story was on the big back table. "Oh, that," she said, in heavily accented English. "That's the Stamtich." Seeing I had no idea what she was talking about, she went on. "It's what you would call in English, the head table. It is where only the senior guys sit."

After a grabbing an old copy of the *Stars and Stripes* newspaper, I headed for one of the many empty tables. It was nice to just relax and enjoy the beer. I was considering having one more of these good beers when my thoughts were interrupted by a loud voice coming from the back of the room. "Hey, kid!" I looked up to see Jimmy Smith looking down the room in my direction and waving me over to the Stamtich.

Jim Smith was one of those legendary characters found in every army unit. Although I had never spoken to him before, I knew him through the many stories I heard about his soldiering abilities. He was reputed to be among the best mortar men in the entire regiment. He had a short, skinny frame with a narrow, wrinkled face. He looked at me through deep-set, half-closed eyes, which gave him the appearance of someone who was about to fall asleep.

He was still smiling when I reached the table, which I took as a good sign, but when I scanned the faces of the other occupants, their demeanour told me that this was perhaps a bad idea. "Come on, take a seat. We don't bite." Judging by the scowls on the other three faces, I had my doubts about his last remark. "This here is Paddy Hays and that guy over there is Albert Dunn," he said, indicating the guys on either side of him. Paddy and I had met a few days earlier in the mess hall. At age fifty, he held the distinction of being the oldest soldier in the battalion. Paddy was a "Career Private" and more than happy to remain so for the rest of his time in the army. He was reputed to have the ear of every senior officer in the entire regiment. Because of his age and status, he could simply walk in to the CO's office as he pleased to discuss any matter he deemed necessary. Paddy's friendly smile gave me some momentary ease as I sat down at the table. "Over there is Chief Powers." Jimmy pointed to the last member of the group, sitting directly across from me. Paddy and Albert reached across in turn and shook my hand. When I stretched my hand over the middle of the table, Chief Powers just sat there, unmoving, and glared at me. After a moment, I withdrew my hand and sat back down, smiling nervously.

"Did you know that Stoney here is Irish?" Paddy asked, breaking the momentary awkward silence.

I felt the pressure was off me as Albert began relating a long-winded story comparing his drinking experiences in Ireland and other European countries. "Don't care what anyone says, nothing beats a pint of Guinness; right, Stoney?" Other than stealing a sip from someone's glass at an Irish hoolie when I was a kid, I had never drank the stuff. However, I was sure that was not the answer Albert wanted to hear, so I just nodded my head in vigorous agreement.

The drunken discussion about beer continued, with Paddy throwing out an opinion about the merits of Harp versus Heineken. I was more of a spectator through all this conversation, but I couldn't fail to notice that Chief Powers had continued to glower in my direction and had not said a single word since I sat down.

I was actually beginning to enjoy myself and about to offer to buy a round, when Powers finally broke his silence with a remark that caught me completely off guard. "Why the fuck weren't you in Korea, boy?" he hissed in my direction. The argument between Paddy and Albert abruptly ended, as both of them turned their attention to me. I sat there in stunned silence, not knowing if the question was serious or some sort of joke at my expense. Paddy and Albert suddenly burst out laughing, and for just a second I thought this was only a joke, but the continued serious expression on the Chief's face told me that it was anything but funny. Chief Powers was one very large Indian, whom I knew by reputation as someone to avoid, especially when he was drinking.

"Well, you know, I really tried to go, but the recruiter told me they weren't taking six year olds that year," I said with a weak smile, trying to make light of his question and hopefully defuse the situation. It didn't work.

"Where do you get off sitting at this table, boy? A young snot like you doesn't have the right to sit here!"

Before I could remind him that I had actually been invited, both Paddy and Jimmy jumped to my defence. "Leave the kid alone, Chief, he ain't bothering you."

As suddenly as it had started, it was over. Powers looked satisfied as he sat back in his chair, snapped his half full bottle of beer up from the table, and drank it down in one long swallow. "Right," he said, slamming the empty back down, "that's enough bullshit for one night. I'm out of here." I tried to look casual and hide my deep sense of relief as he gave me one last glaring stare, got up, and slowly negotiated his way toward the door.

"Not to worry, Stoney," Paddy said as he got out of earshot. "He's just an asshole who can't hold his booze." Within a minute Paddy and Albert were once again completely absorbed in yet another discussion of alcohol, only this time they were touting the merits of various types of rye whiskey.

As the younger crowd started to filter into the battalion, I soon realized that most had the same negative thoughts about the canteen and rarely, if ever, went there. Its reputation as a place of "old" soldiers was clear when you heard the younger soldiers refer to it by various names including "Menopause Manor," "The Elephant Graveyard," or "The Pensioners Club."

At the far end of the building that housed the canteen there was also a small cafeteria, which the majority of the single guys used on a daily basis.

Considering that the prices were generally high and the menu consisted of only the basic staples — like hot dogs, hamburgers, french fries, and Coke — it was rare to go into the place at any time of the day or night and not find it at least half-full of hungry soldiers. At first glance one would find this rather odd, especially when the mess hall was literally steps away and served the standard three meals each day.

All it took for most people to find the answer to this question was to eat their first few meals in the mess hall. The food was simply awful and the service was even worse. The men's mess hall in Fort York had the dubious distinction of having the worst food in the entire brigade. Boiled soggy potatoes, carrots, and some sort of stewing meat was the standard fare. Aside from plates, there were no other utensils provided. We had to bring our own knife, fork, spoon, and even cup. On the frequent occasions when we came for a meal straight from work and did not wish to make the long trip back to the shack for utensils, our only option was to make a sandwich out of whatever was being served that day. For those lucky few who managed to make it to a meal early, there was a small number of peanut butter jars available as drink holders.

The building itself was infested with cockroaches, and we all got into the habit of searching our plates carefully before digging in. One afternoon while I was assigned to work in the kitchen, I spotted a large, fat cockroach darting along the counter. By the time I grabbed the can of insecticide he had succeeded in escaping through a narrow crack that ran the length of the wall. We had been told by the kitchen officer (KO) to just ignore them, but this guy was a big sucker, and, like that prize fish battling at the end of your line, I just had to get him. I held the spray can nozzle against the crack and saturated the entire wall, hoping to force him out into the open for the kill. My efforts to flush him out were actually too successful. Within moments he, along with hundreds, perhaps thousands, of his relatives, came pouring out of the crack. After a minute, a solid black mass covered the area and made the entire wall look like it was alive and moving. It wasn't until this point that I realized that this was probably why the KO had specifically told us to leave them alone. As punishment I was banished to the back of the kitchen for the rest of the week to do the worst job of all.

Some people euphemistically referred to it as "Pearl Diving" or "Pot Walloping," but regardless of what title it was given, it still meant I was elbow deep in greasy water scrubbing pots and pans every night, long after everyone else had finished work.

The number of duties that had to be done each evening far outnumbered the amount of soldiers available to do them. Many evenings were spent on a variety of duties, from guarding the ammunition dump, to fire picket or gate guard. For those nights when you were fortunate enough to be free of duties, there was a movie theatre near the back of the base. For just two marks, which was the equivalent of about fifty cents, you could see a movie and also get popcorn and a soft drink to go along with it. One movie in particular was shown at least once every six months, but never failed to fill every last seat in the place.

The Dam Busters told the true story of the destruction of three massive hydroelectric dams during the Second World War. What made it all the more interesting was having one of these rebuilt dams spanning the waters of the Mohne Sea just three miles away from the base.

On my first trip to visit the Mohne Dam, I remember something I saw on the main road leading down into the valley, which reminded me of just why we were in West Germany. The main road ran through the town of Delika, and once you reached the outskirts of the town the road descended steeply into the western end of the Ruhr Valley. When we reached the valley floor, we came across three major roads, from the north, south, and east, all intersecting at one key junction just below the massive dam. What was immediately noticeable in the middle of this intersection were no less than ten manholes, each spaced evenly apart in a large circle. To see one or even two or three manholes would not be unusual and probably go unnoticed by most people, but to see ten seemed rather odd.

Our German bus driver spoke perfect English and seemed pleased to demonstrate his ability when I asked him about this unusual amount of manholes covering the entire intersection. "Looks like they have a serious drainage problem around here," I said, pointing at all the manholes.

"Trust me," he said smiling, "it has nothing to do with drainage." He went on to explain, as I sat there listening in quiet amazement. "This intersection is one of only a few main arteries into the Ruhr Valley, and the holes are there to destroy the roadway when the Russians come." The fact that he had used the word "when" and not "if" was not lost on me.

By then, everyone on the bus was listening intently. "You see, the holes are specifically designed to take a one-hundred-pound explosive charge. The explosive charge itself looks a lot like a large wheel of cheese, and can be quickly and easily dropped down each hole and all detonated simultaneously, leaving you with one huge crater blocking the entire road." He took a moment to let this sink in and then went on. "Yes, all of the major road junctions, including the Autobahn highways and all the bridges built since the end of the war were designed for rapid destruction when the time comes."

Newcomers like us may have had our doubts about what the future held, but many of the German people, especially the older ones, still harboured vivid memories of the Red Army. The war may have ended twenty years earlier, but to the Germans the threat was still very real.

Chapter 3
Of Mice and Men

It had taken almost six weeks, but by the end of November the majority of the battalion, including most of my friends from basic training, were finally on the ground in Fort York. The good news for me was there were now enough single men available to take their turn at cleaning the barracks. I could at last go back to normal training.

Winter came early that year, and by mid November we had our first dusting of snow. Unlike Canada, we rarely received more than a trace of the white stuff, but the sleet and rain was another matter. Throughout November and well into December we seemed to have unending days of cold, biting rain and winds that cut straight through and chilled us to the very bone.

The one bright light during this first dreary winter was hockey. At first we went to the Fort York Arena just simply to have something to do on those long cold winter nights, but we soon became swept up in the excitement and the electric atmosphere of the place. The Royals were a good team, and the majority of its members were newly arrived from Canada. The calibre of hockey was exceptionally high throughout the six teams, which made up the Brigade League.

Every game became an event, with people crowding into the arena long before puck drop. The long, low, metal roof of the building helped amplify the shouts and screams of the boisterous crowd. Each team had their own unique method of signaling a goal. For the Royals, it was a .30-calibre machinegun set up immediately behind the boards in the opponents' end of the rink. When the Royals scored, the roar of the home crowd would be accompanied by the ear-splitting sound of an entire belt of blank ammunition being pumped through the machinegun. The Gunners, from the artillery regiment, had a miniature cannon at every game, and when they scored a goal the deafening roar of cannon fire would echo and vibrate throughout the entire building.

All of the games were eagerly anticipated, but none more so than when the home team took on their most vicious opponents — the Princess Patricia

Canadian Light Infantry (PPCLI). I don't know for sure why the animosity was so great between the two groups, but I had heard a story about an incident a couple of years earlier, which may have been the spark that ignited the fire. The story was that one of the Patricia hockey players had been caught in bed with another soldier. Regardless of whether the story was true or not, the rumours quickly spread throughout the entire brigade. One dark night, two RCR soldiers had apparently strung a large sign on the fence just outside the Patricia camp. The sign read "Welcome to Fruitland." The CO of the PPCLI then sent a nasty letter to the CO of the RCR, obviously complaining about the sign and its clearly implied message. The commanding officer of the RCR in turn sent a package and a letter of apology to his PPCLI counterpart. If the story is at all true, this is probably what started the ongoing feud. Aside from the letter, the package also contained a large fruitcake. Considering the army of the 1960s was a completely male-dominated, homophobic society, I believe there is probably some particle of truth hidden somewhere in the story.

Regardless of what the reasons were, all the games between the Royals and the Pats were always fight-filled events. You could be guaranteed at least two or three brawls in every game. On more than one occasion, the fights actually spilled over into the stands and the game would be delayed while the MPs escorted the combatants out of the building and into a cell.

My friends and I may have been among the staunched team supporters, but I have to admit that many of us, including myself, were somewhat jealous of the preferential treatment the team members received, even when they were off the ice. They were rarely, if ever, put on any of the more mundane duties the rest of us peons had to perform, such as kitchen fatigues, gate guard, or fire picket. At supper time on game night, they would all sit together in the mess hall and be served a nice juicy steak, while the rest of us could only get stew.

Even the stringent code of military discipline was applied with a good deal more leniency when it came to hockey players. During an exercise in Northern Germany we had been given the evening off, so most of the soldiers headed into the nearby town of Soltau. The majority of both anti-tank platoon and mortar platoon ended up crowding into one tiny *gasthof*, which is a German inn or hotel with a bar. The single waitress could not keep up with the crush of customers, all yelling to be served. A fight soon broke out between a couple of guys from the opposing platoons. It took no time at all for this one fight to erupt into a full-blown riot. About forty guys threw tables, chairs, glasses, and anything else that wasn't nailed down. By the time the military police and the duty officer arrived, the gasthof was a shambles and there were numerous bloodied bodies strewn about the floor.

The duty officer was a big, strapping German-Canadian we all called "The Hun." He had a reputation as a no-nonsense type of officer who had no compunction about throwing soldiers in jail, even for the most minor of offences. He came through the gasthof door and right into the centre of the floor, with prostate bodies lying all around him. "Right!" he screamed. "Everyone here can now consider themselves on charge and you are all going to jail!" Lying right at his feet was Les McNally, one of the biggest guys in anti-tank platoon. As Les told me later, "I knew I was going to jail anyway, so I just figured I may as well make it worthwhile." In less than a second, McNally came straight up off the floor and caught The Hun full in the jaw with a vicious right hook, sending him crashing to the floor like a sack of potatoes. Once we returned to Fort York, Les was brought before the CO on the very serious charge of striking a superior officer. The colonel had little choice other than to sentence him to sixty days detention. Serious charges such as this also carried the almost automatic punishment of being dishonourably discharged from the military once the jail sentence was complete.

Had Private McNally been an average soldier, the story would end here, with him being shipped off to the field detention barracks near Fort Henry to complete his sentence, and then returned to Canada for release. Les and I served many years together and he was a very conscientious, hardworking individual, but he was certainly no ordinary soldier. He was not only a hockey player, but the best forward on the entire battalion team. To make matters worse, the playoffs were about to begin, and if the Royals were to have any change at all of getting to the finals, Les would have to play.

Les did serve his sentence, but was kept in the guardroom so he could be close to the hockey arena. Each morning he would appear in his black prisoner coveralls and an MP would march him down the road, swinging his left arm, with his kit bag that was full of hockey equipment slung over his right shoulder. During the game, the MPs would stand guard behind the players' bench. Once the game ended, he would shower and change back into coveralls for the short march back to his jail cell.

The Royals lost in the finals that year. After serving just forty-five days of his sixty day sentence, Les was let out for good behaviour. The mandatory release from the military never happened and he continued to serve well into the late 1970s.

Those feelings of resentment we ordinary soldiers had toward hockey players was also extended to include those elite few who received special treatment for being a member of the battalion baseball team, soccer team, or even the battalion track and field team. The common term we used to lump them all together was "Jock Strappers." Most of them certainly had the talent to be where they were, but our resentment stemmed from the fact that while we were busy doing all the work they did little other than practice their sport. If the definition of a professional athlete is "one who gets paid for completion in a sport," these guys fit the requirement exactly.

• • •

The "liquid sunshine" of Northern Germany continued unabated throughout November and long into December. The mood in the quarters was as bitter and sombre as the slate-grey sky we woke up to each morning. The few radiators spread along the inside wall of our shack gave heat to only those fortunate enough to be within a ten-foot radius. The rest of us just piled on the extra blankets we had managed to scrounge from the quartermaster.

If the winter was harsh for us, it was quite catastrophic for the camp's rodent population. By early October, we had all become aware of a noticeable increase in the field mouse population of the base. Whether walking to or from work, the mess hall, or anywhere in camp, it was not unusual to see hundreds of mice scurrying in all directions. Because of the sheer numbers, it became an effort to actually avoid stepping on them. We had been told that this increase was the direct result of a virtual extinction of their main enemy, the European Red Fox. With this predator gone, nature's balance was upset, and in no time at all the number of field mice exploded into a teeming mass.

Initially, the problem was not too bad indoors because the weather stayed relatively mild throughout October. The real plague began by mid November, when the cold temperatures and incessant rain forced these rodents to seek shelter.

The little buggers were everywhere! You couldn't open a locker or a barrack box without seeing three or four scurrying about, looking for food and warmth. Even getting into bed at night took some time. You had to pull back all the sheets and blankets and lift the mattress, all in a vain effort to clear them away. While the lights were on they were somewhat manageable because they would at least run for cover. However, once you finally settled down for the night and turned out the lights, you could immediately hear them swarming about in the darkness. Although they certainly presented a health hazard because of their tiny droppings, I don't believe they were all that dangerous. In the month or so that the invasion lasted, I never heard of anyone being bitten or otherwise being injured by these tiny rodents. This, however, did not prevent a lot of people, including me, from jumping out of bed in the middle of the night with frightened screams because one or more of these little buggers had run across your face.

I have read some serious studies about what it is that turns men into serial killers. Many of the experts have said that their careers may start in early childhood by killing small animals. If this were true, there definitely was a bumper crop of serial killers being created in Fort York that year.

Every shack had two or three large iron floor polishers. They were simple devices made up of a broom handle with a very heavy metal piece on the bottom. A cloth or rag was placed under the bottom and used to manually buff the floors. Their sheer weight made them the weapon of choice for many fighting the rodent war. All you had to do was stand over one of the many cracks in the walls or drains in the floor, and when the enemy appeared, he could be easily squashed under the weight of the polisher. For many, this method took far too much patience because you had to stand there with the polisher dangling over the hole waiting for your prey, and even then you only got one mouse. Although it was severely frowned upon by the fire marshal, many of the more aggressive guys preferred the silicone blowtorch to get a higher ratio of kills in a shorter period of time. I am quite sure that when the military provided us with spray cans of silicone to waterproof out coats and boots, they had no idea we could come up with more inventive uses for these pressurized cans.

Again the method was simple, albeit a little bit dangerous. All you had to do was hold a lit match in front of the spray, and it would instantly erupt into an extremely effective flame thrower. Of course you had to be quick and keep the fire bursts short or there was always the danger that if the flame were held too long, it could back up into the can and explode in your hand. To the best of my knowledge, this never happened, but there were a number of minor accidents involving the loss of eye brows and moustaches when a user got too close to the source of the flame. This method also produced some other problems, particularly when a soldier went to the quartermaster stores trying to explain why he needed to exchange a blanket or sheet or some article of clothing because they had burn or singe marks.

Despite all of our inventiveness, the mouse population never seemed to decrease. Even when we found ways to increase the efficiency by combining different killing methods, the plague raged on.

When it came to fighting these rodents, we did have one pacifist in our midst, or at least I thought he was, until he did something really bizarre one night. It still makes me cringe when I think about it.

Chuck McIssac was a rather strange little guy who was friendly enough but always appeared to be a death's door. He was only in his thirties, but already had the first signs of grey in his receding hairline. He had a sallow complexion, with dark, sunken eyes. When he removed his shirt, every single rib was easily distinguishable on his skeleton-like frame. Chuck was an alcoholic. The odd thing is that nobody seemed to care. He was, without doubt, a good worker, which I assumed at the time was the reason why he was left alone. As long as he showed up and worked each day, no one was going to confront him about his problem.

His life seemed to be one continuous drinking cycle. Each evening he would head straight for the canteen, rarely stopping to eat more than a sandwich at the mess hall. When the canteen closed, he would head for Lucy's Gasthof, right outside the front gate, pick up a half chicken, stagger back to his bed space, and devour most of the chicken before passing out on his bed.

Whenever one of us got up during the night, we would automatically check on him. If he was passed out on his back, we would roll him on his side or onto his stomach and make sure the fire bucket was close by for his almost nightly bouts of vomiting. His usual morning routine consisted of throwing up in the toilet, followed by a quick shower and shave. I would watch him get dressed, make his bed, and head out the door at the last possible moment for morning parade. Just before leaving, I would often see him take some mysterious bottle from his locker and take a quick swig while trying to remain hidden behind the door.

One night, at the height of the rodent wars, a couple of the guys and I decided to head for the movies. After sitting through some forgettable western, we headed for Lucy's to treat ourselves to some chicken and chips, and perhaps a beer or two. No sooner had we come through the door and placed our order, when I spotted Chuck at the far corner table. He appeared to be in the middle of a very animated conversation. I became a little concerned because I could see the entire barroom, and he was sitting alone with no one else close by. "Everything all right, Chuck?" my friends and I asked, approaching the table.

Chuck gave us a momentary vacant stare before finally recognizing us. "What are you kids doing up so late," he said and laughed. Chuck always talked to my friends and me as if he was a father figure and we were the kids. He had been doing it from the first day I walked into the shack, and he always seemed to find the whole concept hilarious. Once I told him we were waiting for some chicken, he told us to take a seat. As soon as we sat down, I realized who he had been talking to earlier. Sticking out of his shirt pocket was a tiny field mouse, which Chuck was feeding small pieces of french fry. "I want to introduce you to the new kid on the block," he announced, gently reaching into his pocket and putting the mouse on his plate. "I want you kids to meet your new brother, Fitzgerald."

"Hey Fitz, how are you doing?" we all chimed back, playing along with the little game. Obviously the mouse didn't understand the game, because he continued to nibble away at the leftover french fries on Chuck's plate.

"Where are your manners Fitzgerald? Say hello to your brothers." After a moment without a response, Chuck became visibly angry, scooping the mouse up into to his fist. "I said to say hello, you little shit!" Chuck held the mouse at arm's length, with its tiny head sticking out just above the thumb of his clenched fist. Just when I thought it couldn't possibly get any more bizarre, it happened. "Think you can ignore me, you ungrateful little prick?" In one quick motion, Chuck shoved the hapless mouse into his mouth and bit its head clean off.

For just a split second we all sat in stunned silence, but once we saw the blood jetting out of the headless torso and looked at Chuck, who was smiling with bits of mouse skin protruding from his open mouth, we immediately jumped up, knocking over the chairs and table in the process. Thankfully, at least he didn't swallow the creature, but after a little chewing, he finally spat it out onto the floor. The few people who had witnessed the savagery all made for the exit. The bar owner was truly upset and came over, demanding that we all leave. We were more than happy to comply.

Later that night, while trying to get the image out of my head and fall asleep, I overheard Chuck mumbling away in his bed space. "I want you to behave and go to sleep. That's a good boy." I smiled to myself, realizing that Chuck was already over the untimely death of Fitzgerald and had captured a new mouse friend.

After a couple of days we all noticed that the new mouse had disappeared, but no one was about to ask Chuck what had happened. We all just assumed that Fitzgerald number two had somehow offended Chuck and had met the same savage end as his predecessor. News of Chuck's strange eating habits spread throughout the camp, and soon everyone started referring to Chuck by a new nickname. For the remainder of his short life, he would always be known as "Chewy McIssac."

On a cold winter's morning in 1968, after a marathon weekend of drinking, Chewy was found dead in his bed. Later that same day, the company commander had everyone in the shack gathered together in the main hallway. We all assumed correctly that it was to tell us Chewy's official cause of death. After falling asleep on his back, he had choked to death in his own vomit. The sombre mood we all felt soon turned to anger, as the company commander went on. "I blame each and every one of you," he said, as his eyes swept across the group. "You should have taken better care of him." He abruptly walked out, leaving the accusation hanging in the air. I can't say what the others felt about what had been said, but for me the feeling was a mixture of remorse and anger. Yes, someone should have, could have, rolled him onto his stomach for the thousandth time, but why didn't those in charge do something to help him with his drinking problem when it had been so obvious for so long?

The war of mice and men dragged on into the latter part of November, but we could see that we were slowly gaining the upper hand. Our victory was not the result of using such sophisticated weapons as floor polishers or silicone brow torches, but rather the combined effects of toxic spray and the weather.

One morning on first parade, we were dispatched to work and told to stay clear of the quarters for the entire day while all the buildings were fumigated. When we were finally allowed to return that evening, the smell of whatever spray had been used was almost overwhelming, but there wasn't a single live mouse anywhere to be found. After gingerly disposing of the dead carcasses, we could finally throw open all the window and doors and breathe in the cold fresh air. The few mice who had managed to escape to the outside would soon succumb to the bitter winter cold. By mid December, the rodents had disappeared. The war was over and we had won, albeit with a little help from science and Mother Nature.

• • •

Just before Christmas, Sergeant Stoke called me into his office to give me the long-awaited news. The pioneer course would be starting early in the New Year, and I was on it. Being that this would be my first Christmas away from home,

I certainly was not looking forward to the holidays, but at least now, I thought, I could keep my mind busy by increasing my study time for the course.

Christmas Eve was another in a long line of dull, overcast days. Fort York was practically deserted, as with all of the married men being given the entire holiday week off, only we single soldiers remained on the base. Aside from the canteen, all the base facilities were shut down tight and would remain that way until after Boxing Day. The traditional men's Christmas dinner had been done earlier in the week, but the cooks, with their usual lack of imagination, were still serving leftover turkey and ham for almost every meal. After a lacklustre supper of hot turkey sandwiches and boiled potatoes, I returned to the shack with the intent of reading my way through the mine warfare manual, while most of my roommates were busy boozing it up in the canteen.

I read an entire chapter before realizing that I had not, in fact, taken in a single word. I started over again, at the beginning, but my mind kept wandering to thoughts of my family. It would be roughly noon, on Christmas Eve, in Toronto. Would my ten-year-old brother Philip be excitedly preparing for Santa to arrive that night? Would my sister Rose be busy cooking a turkey and checking the Christmas puddings she had made for tomorrow's dessert? Would my Dad be working this night, as he so often had to do? My anger at being thrown out had long passed and I just hoped that he could finally find a little happiness, on this the fourth Christmas since my mother's death.

By eight o'clock I knew I was getting nowhere with my reading, but it was too early to try and sleep. Before I could make up my mind what to do, the decision was made for me. "So this is where you're hiding!" Joe Payton and Larry Dooley shouted excitedly, as they came storming through the door. I tried making some excuse about having to study, but in their drunken state they were not buying it. Larry told me that he and Joe, along with three or four of the guys, had gone to the canteen for a few beers after supper. "We tried turning up the music and having a little fun, but you know what those old farts are like," he went on in disgust. "All those cranky old buggers want to do is sit around and tell war stories and give us a hard time." I remembered well what had happened to me the first time I had gone in and clearly understood why anyone under the ripe old age of thirty would not feel at all welcome in "Menopause Manor."

After a little more discussion, I fished around the bottom of my barrack box, pulling out the well-hidden bottle of Canadian Club. After each taking a swig, we all headed next door to find the rest of the guys. By nine o'clock, there were six of us, with an equal number of bottles, all sitting in Larry Dooley's bed space and all at various stages of drunkenness.

I have absolutely no memory of what happened after about midnight. I don't know how I got there, but at seven o'clock Christmas morning I awoke to find myself back in my own building, and all curled up with a pillow and blanket on the bench in the shower room.

It took me two full days to recover, but by the time New Year's rolled around, I was back to my old self. I finally buckled down to study and was quite proud of the fact that I had read all of the course reference material by the time normal work recommenced in January.

This was the first, but certainly would not be the last time, I suffered through a serious hangover. This Christmas drinking binge had only cost me a couple of sick days, as well as a weeklong backache from sleeping on a wooden bench. Little did I know that the Christmas of 1966 would find me sleeping behind bars, all because of someone else's alcohol abuse.

Chapter 4
The Perils of Peanut Butter and Jam

We all sat there in the classroom looking around apprehensively at our competition for the few available spots in pioneer platoon. We had been warned that of the thirty candidates in the room, only the top five would be going to the platoon.

I had done relatively well on the anti-tank course some six months earlier, but there had been just one subject to master. If you learned all there was to know about the 106 mm recoilless rifles, from stripping, assembling, cleaning, and firing the weapon successfully, you could pass this course in four to five weeks. The assault pioneer course was to be an intense eight weeks of mastering a large variety of totally different subjects, from mine warfare, to field geometry, to bridging, to watermanship, to the most difficult subject of all: demolitions.

As I sat in the lecture room that first morning, I was fully aware that this was going to be one of those defining moments in my life. My options were very limited. I felt confident that my weeks of studying had given me enough knowledge to pass the course, but getting into that top five would be a daunting task. As I scanned the room I could see that there were a fair number of smart, intelligent individuals who were certainly going to give me a good run for my money.

Those first two weeks were a long and arduous grind. Hour after hour was spent in the classroom learning the theory and principles of everything from the amount of energy created from an exploding charge, to the mechanism used to detonate an anti-personnel and anti-tank mines, and the most accurate methods of measuring the speed of the current in a fast-flowing river.

Probably one of the most interesting lessons was on the use of booby trap switches. Like most people who had ever watched a war movie, I had thought that a booby trap was something which was just some improvised device which was thrown together at the last minute to catch an unsuspecting enemy, when in fact there were a number of mechanical devices specifically designed for this very purpose.

We all sat listening intently as the instructor explained that practically all booby trap switches worked on four basic principles: pull, pressure, or delay. If, for example, you used a door and the knob was connected to a trip wire running to an explosive charge, once anyone attempted to open the door, the "pull" on the trip wire would fire the detonator inside the booby trap switch, and this would instantaneously detonate the explosive charge inside. If the device were placed under the leg of a chair, once anyone sat down, the weight and downward "pressure" would cause the explosion. Similarly, if you placed the device under some heavy object, like a phone book, the "release" of pressure once the book was lifted would detonate the device. The last method of "delay" was the simplest of all. Each switch comes with a tag indicating a given amount of delay time before the device will detonate. The inside of the switch contained a metal rod which was surrounded by a glass vile, containing corrosive acid. All one would have to do was bury the switch and explosive charge in a floor or wall and simply remove the safety pin just before departing. Once the pin is removed, the acid is released and imme-diately starts eating its way through the metal rod. The rods are of various thicknesses, dependent upon the elapsed time required, so the acid can take as little as one hour or as long as a week to burn through the rod, thereby firing the explosive charge.

From the very first lesson we received on booby traps, the instructor immediately got our full attention. We had just taken our seats in the class-room after lunch when the instructor introduced himself by setting off a rather loud gunpowder charge at the front of the room. If that wasn't enough to get our undivided attention, he next announced that there were similar charges set throughout the entire room. Hardly had he gotten the words out of his mouth, when one of the guys detonated another of the training charges after lifting a stack of books from his desk. A cloud of white smoke filled the room, so the instructor told me to open the door at the back of the room. Not thinking, I quickly jumped out of my seat and pulled the door open, which set off yet another big bang of gunpowder. By the time the last of the smoke dissipated, we were all quite paranoid, afraid to make even the slightest movement. After a prolonged pause, the instructor finally spoke. "Gentlemen, you have just learned the first principle of booby traps: TRUST NOTHING — SUSPECT EVERYTHING!"

By the time the eighty-minute lesson ended, another six or seven explo-sions had rattled through the classroom. Like most, I had been taking notes throughout the lecture, but later on I had a hard time deciphering my writing because of the scrawls I had across the page every time we had a fresh explosion. He finished his lecture with one of the most colourful summaries I had ever heard given in a military lesson. "Gentlemen," he said, "I have just covered the principles of booby trapping and you can rest assured that it will be a question on the final test. If you have trouble remembering these principles, just think about masturbation." If we weren't listening before, we certainly were then. He paused to let this word sink in. "At your age, when you masturbate you 'pull,' which causes 'pressure,' which leads to a 'release,' but sometimes, as you get older, you can experience a 'delay.'" I completed the pioneer course over forty years ago, but I never forgot those principles.

Every couple of days we had a quickie test on all the material covered up to that point in the course. These tests usually came first thing in the morning and were geared to wake you up and get the brain working. By the end of week two we had completed six of these tests and I was holding my own at a 96 percent overall average. During this early theoretical stage of the course, Andy Bolski was proving to be my stiffest competition. During those frequent quickie tests I would sneak a sideways glance in his direction and there he would be writing away, with barely a pause to reflect on the questions. He just had that look of supreme confidence as if to say that these questions were just too easy and hardly worthy of his attention. Invariably, when we returned from lunch and checked the test results posted on the notice board, our two names would be at the top of the page.

Andy was one of those unique individuals who seemed to sail through life, without a care in the world. As the saying goes, he definitely marched to the beat of a different drum. He had a short, rotund body, with a head that always appeared too large for his stunted frame. Although he was just past twenty, his hairline was already showing signs of rapid receding. A thin, dark, pencil-like moustache was in stark contrast to his otherwise very pale facial features.

Usually by seven o'clock I was well into my evening routine of studying when Andy would breeze by my bed space, heading for Lucy's Bar and a cab downtown. Our next sighting of him would be at breakfast, where he would regale us with stories of drunken debauchery and how he had managed to charm yet another gorgeous female right into the sack.

Regardless of the ongoing competition between us, Andy and I were friends. I didn't begrudge him his seemingly effortless ability to do well on these written tests. It did not take long to figure out that he was an extremely intelligent individual, who had that innate ability to grasp and hold ideas and concepts instantly, while the rest of us mere mortals had to struggle just to reach some level of understanding.

I was well aware that Sunday afternoon, as I strained to wrap my mind around the dry and boring subject of explosives, that there would no doubt be a quickie test on all this first thing tomorrow. I was so intent on my reading it took me a couple of minutes to realize that Andy was standing there lazily leaning against my locker, waiting for me to notice him. "What are you up to?" His presence momentarily startled me.

"Trying to figure out what the hell they are talking about here!" I said, stabbing my finger at the section of the book titled *The Principles of Explosives*.

Andy looked rather bored as he continued to lean against my locker. "I wouldn't worry about that shit. It's pretty straightforward." Andy and I may have been on friendly terms, but his condescending attitude was beginning to piss me off.

"Okay, smartass," I quickly scanned the page looking for a question I could stump him with. "What is the definition of explosive detonation?"

He looked at me for only a moment, took a slow drag off his cigarette before speaking. "That would be 'the instantaneous rearrangement of molecules caused by the displacement of great amounts of energy.'" I couldn't help but be amazed by his ability to actually quote the book exactly. The guy was a freak of nature. "It's no big deal. I just read the words once and remember."

"Now I get it!" I said, suddenly understanding, "you have a photographic memory."

"I'd rather have a pornographic memory," he laughed. "Now that would be a lot more fun." He butted his cigarette out on the already dirty floor. "Trust me, Stoney, you're far better off putting in the time studying the course material. I can quote the words verbatim, right out of the book, but that doesn't mean I truly grasp their meaning. It may take you longer, but in the end at least you'll have a far better understanding than me." I had absolutely no idea what to say to this, so I said nothing.

After four unending weeks in the classroom, the theory portion of the course was over. Although we still had a lot of practical work to do to pass the pioneer course, we were all more than happy to be boarding a truck for the long ride to the training area and our first real experience with live explosives.

After two hours of bitter cold in the back of a truck, the initial enthusiasm of finally being out of the classroom quickly wore off. When the tailgate dropped, it took only seconds for us all to dismount and gratefully jump about in an effort to try and get some feeling back into our frozen bodies.

The first order of business was to get the trucks unloaded and set up our base camp for the next four days. Normally the work would have taken the better part of an entire day, but as the platoon sergeant back in basic training had drummed into us so often, "The best way to stay warm when working outdoors in winter is to stay active!" By mid afternoon the tents for the kitchen, the staff, and students' living quarters, plus all the stores and equipment, were complete. By three o'clock we could see steam emanating from the canvas roof of the kitchen tent as the cook busied himself making supper.

After the mandatory safety briefing the following morning, we all took our turn filing by the ammunition storage area to pick up everything necessary to make our first basic charge. I gingerly accepted the one-pound stick of 808 plastic explosives, and held it firmly against the side of my body. We had been told repeatedly that the explosive charge was perfectly safe to handle, and even if we inadvertently dropped it on the ground it would not detonate. Only a sudden severe shock would cause this charge to go off. We knew all this, but as I looked around, all I could see were the looks of quiet apprehension on each student's face as he received his small explosive package along with a length of safety fuse.

Lastly we were handed a rather innocuous-looking metal cylinder, which was about two inches long, and smaller in diameter than a pencil. The detonator only contained about an ounce of liquid explosive, but it was enough to supply the shock necessary to trigger the main explosive. The detonator may have been tiny, but its liquid explosive was relatively unstable. We were all well aware that it could explode if accidently dropped or even if it were held too long in a warm, closed hand. We each held our stick of 808 and safety fuse firmly in one hand, while carefully holding this little silver cylinder between the thumb and index fingers of the other hand.

Next came the tricky part. After moving out into the middle of the field firing range, we each picked a flat spot and placed our deadly little package down. The explosive plastic was first unwrapped and moulded into a round ball. On a warm day this would be quite easy because a plastic explosive has the same soft consistency as putty, but with today's cold, damp weather, it was like trying to knead cement. To add to our difficulty, we had to do the work while wearing gloves. This particular plastic explosive contained a highly poisonous cyanide substance which, if ingested through the skin, could and certainly would make you seriously ill. By the end of this first training week, I would learn firsthand just how true this was.

After fifteen minutes of hard work, I had managed to mould my plastic into what looked like an oversized softball. Once the instructor approved my creation, I took out my pocket knife and gently pushed the blade into the top of the charge, making a shallow hole. With the plastic ball set off to the side, I completed the next delicate step, under the close scrutiny of the instructor. With the safety fuse held out in front of me, I carefully inserted it into the open end of the detonator. I next took the crimping pliers and squeezed until both were firmly bonded together. It was imperative that these two devices were tight together so that the gun powder from the fuse was right up against the liquid explosive in the head of the detonator.

The three feet of safety fuse gave us well over two minutes to walk away to a safe covered area. After the fuse was lit, it was a simple chain reaction. The gun powder slowly burned down the length of the fuse. Once the flame reached the detonator, it would explode and instantaneously set off the main explosive charge.

It was a long, cold first day of training, but as the late afternoon shadows crept in we had successfully completed that all important first phase of live training. Amazingly we had only two misfires the entire day. After the mandatory thirty-minute wait time for each, the instructor and the poor unfortunate who had put the charge together headed out to see what had gone wrong. In most cases the misfire was the result of the detonator and fuse not being tightly together. Regardless of what the problem is, the solution is the same. The misfired charge is never touched or moved in any way. Instead, a new, larger charge is placed immediately beside the old one, so that when it explodes, both will go off in one much bigger explosion. By five o'clock only a faint amount of daylight remained, as the two guilty individuals headed down range to set off another charge. A few minutes later we heard the sweet sound of two explosions and knew our day was finally over.

That night, in our hastily constructed tent canteen, we all jeered and applauded loudly as the two guilty culprits made their way toward the bar to pay the traditional price for screwing up: one beer per instructor.

By mid week we had moved far beyond simple basic charges. The amount of explosives used was steadily increased as we learned the best methods of attacking a variety of hard targets. For the initial one-pound charge, on open ground, we were only required to move back just over one hundred yards for safety, but as the explosive charges increased and the type of target changed, so too must the safety space involved. Day four drew to a close as we all stood impatiently waiting for the detonation of what would be the biggest explosion we had seen to date.

We had spent the better part of an entire afternoon moulding and then attaching a whole series of 808 plastic explosive charges to a massive steel beam. All of us busied ourselves attaching our individual charges to the target. It was a particularly cold day, which made the job of moulding the 808 more difficult and time consuming. After finally attaching the explosive to the metal, I tried, without success, to pry a small recess in the bottom of the charge to insert the detonator. Finally in frustration, I pulled out my pocket knife and managed to slice a small hole in the base of the explosive. As I finished my delicate task of securing the explosive to the metal, I raised my hand, indicating to the instructor in charge that my work was ready for inspection. The corporal leaned over the beam, scrutinizing my efforts. Finally he stepped back, paused a moment before speaking. "You are good to go." I was quite pleased with myself and feeling more than a little cocky, but as I started to walk away, his next words froze me in my tracks. "Right, Burke. Seeing as you were the first one finished, you get the honour of connecting everything together and firing the charge." Another ten minutes went by before all the individual charges were inspected and approved.

I could feel the corporal breathe on my neck and lean over my shoulder, watching every move I made. After stringing out a fifty foot length of explosive detonating cord along the entire length of the steel beam, I had to tape each of the explosive charges to this main line. In order for this to work, the cords from the charge and the main line had to be very tightly bound together. By the time I reached the fourth or fifth charge, I was sweating profusely from the exerting of trying to ensure that each connection was as tight and as precise as possible. More than twenty minutes had elapsed since I had started this delicate work, and I could see the corporal was beginning to become impatient. As I continued down the line, he would inspect my last connecting and mumble something about having to go faster. I continued to ignore him and concentrate on the task at hand. With the last of the connections tightly taped, only one task remained. Once I had the detonator and six feet of gunpowder fuse firmly bound to the detonating cord, I carefully lit the end and started the long walk back to safety. All of the charges were hooked together with detonating cord so that all would fire together as one massive 200-pound explosion.

From our protective cover, some 550 yards away, we all held our breath waiting for those final few seconds to tick by. Those moments can seem like an eternity, as all sorts of negative thoughts raced through my mind. "Damn it to hell." I muttered under my breath. Why was this taking so long? I could already picture myself nervously walking back out to the unexploded charge when suddenly the air was filled with an immense thunderous crack, followed instantly by a huge column of flames and thick black smoke shooting into the air. Tiny shards of metal made a whistling sound as they flew straight up and then almost instantly fell back to earth. In less than five seconds, it was over. The silence returned. As we stood up from our protective cover, the dust began to settle over the target area and the black cloud was quickly dissipating into the atmosphere.

Our fifth and final day in the field was spent on the mundane job of cleaning up the mess we had made throughout the preceding days. The two-hundred-pound explosion from the previous day had taken only scant seconds to detonate, but it took us the better part of the morning to gather up all the bigger chunks of metal and fill in the massive hole we had created. Just before noon the store's truck sounded its horn, calling us back to the kitchen for some much-needed hot coffee and sandwiches before our long ride home.

By one o'clock we were well on our way back to Fort York. The canvas tarp offered little protection from the biting wind, which swept through the back of the truck as we sped down the highway. The ride had started out well enough for me, but soon after we left the training area, I began to feel a wave of nausea overtake me. An hour into the trip, I was kneeling on the floor at the back of the truck with my head pounding in pain while I vomited over the tailgate. I truly believed I was about to die.

There is an old saying in the army: "If you want sympathy, you can find it between shit and syphilis in the dictionary." Because most army guys associate throwing up with over indulgence in alcohol, at first my steady stream of puking and heaving only brought cheers and jeers. "Come on, Burke you can do better than that. Let's see some real projectile puke! Bet you can't hit the windshield of that car behind us!" After a few minutes, the non-stop puking seemed to subside as I sat back on the cold metal floor, trying to get my bearings. My head still pounded, but at least I could breathe without gagging. At last someone reached down laughing, as he helped me back into a seat. His callous laughter suddenly stopped as he looked down at the front of my parka. As I looked down I immediately saw the reason for his concern. Blood and spit covered my chin and dribbled down the front of my coat. Someone finally banged on the small window separating the cab from the back of the truck and the driver pulled the truck to the side of the road. The corporal was suitably upset for the interruption to his nap in the front of the truck. "This better be good," he ranted as he came around the side of the truck. His demeanour changed instantly as he took in the scene of my distress.

There wasn't a lot anyone could do for me. A small group such as ours did not rate a medic travelling with them. We were in the middle of nowhere and all we had was a first aid kit. After a few minutes of indecision the corporal decided that the best bet was to carry on back to base, as quickly as possible. I stretched out on the hard, wood bench seat in the back, as the truck flew even faster down the road toward home.

The late afternoon winter sky was beginning to turn grey as we drove through the front gate of Fort York. It was just past five o'clock as the truck pulled to a stop in front of the small medical office. Other than the guard on the front gate, the entire place looked deserted. A handwritten sign on the office door told us that the duty medic was at supper and would be back in thirty minutes.

Other than a persistent banging headache, I was beginning to feel a little better. I managed to make it out of the back of the truck with some assistance, and was happy just to be off that moveable wind tunnel and back on solid ground. I must have looked a sorry sight, as I steadied myself against the side of the truck. The corporal had sent a runner to the officer's mess, looking for the medical officer. By then all of the guys had bailed out of the truck and most were just jumping around, trying to get some warmth back into their arms and legs. "How are you doing?" The corporal asked me for the third time since we stopped.

"I'm okay," I said, trying to smile. This was true, but as I looked around me I was beginning to feel a little guilty. Other than coffee and some cold jam sandwiches, none of us had anything to eat since six o'clock that morning. "Corporal, shouldn't the guys get to supper before the mess hall closes?" No one had to be told twice as everyone jumped back aboard the truck and headed for the mess hall, a scant twenty minutes before the door would close for the night.

The doctor was a young captain who had only been with the battalion for less than a month. Judging by his first question, I assumed he was not too pleased about having his dinner interrupted. "How much did you have to drink last night?" He may have been an officer and a doctor, but I had a hard time disguising the fact that his question pissed me off.

"By drink, if you mean coffee, I had two cups this morning and one last night. If you mean Coke, I had one after supper last night. If you mean water, I had some in the truck this afternoon. If you mean alcohol, I had one beer four days ago, Sir." I think my obvious sarcasm caught him off guard, but at this point, my head was still pounding and I didn't much care that my smart ass reply to a captain could get me charged with insubordination.

The doc just stared at me for a few seconds before finally speaking. "Okay, strip to the waist and lie down over there," he said, pointing to his examination table.

After a few minutes of poking and prodding my stomach, he had me roll over and began tapping on my back. There were no more glib remarks as he continued his examination. Other than a nagging headache, I was beginning to feel much better, but the silence, coupled with the serious expression on his face, was making me quite nervous. I tried telling him I was feeling better, but he cut me off in mid sentence. "Just a second," he said as he sat down and started scribbling down notes on a medical pad. After some minutes, he broke the silence with a question. "What did you have to eat today?"

"A peanut butter and jam sandwich," I replied.

At last he stopped writing and turned to me with a look of satisfaction stretched across his face. "You have all the signs of food poisoning," he said flatly. Seeing the concern on my face, he quickly continued. "Not to worry. The fact that you threw up probably means that whatever it was is now out of your system."

I felt better for just a moment, then another thought struck me. "That can't be right, doc. Everybody had the same thing and none ..." Before I could finish speaking the answer suddenly struck me.

That morning, after the clean up, we had all crowded around the tailgate of the truck trying to make a sandwich to hold us over for the long trip home. There were only a couple of knives available and a long lineup trying to get at them. After a long hungry wait, I was growing impatient, so, not thinking, I pulled out my pocket knife and used it to spread the peanut butter and jam onto the bread.

It had taken only a split second to fully comprehend just what had happened. I sat there with my mouth open, staring at this young doctor and wondering if I should tell him the truth. I had used the knife to cut into the 808 explosive and it obviously had some minuscule particles remaining on it when I made the sandwich. I had cyanide poisoning! The question that sped through my still aching head was whether or not to tell the doctor. I quickly weighed my options as he continued to stare at me, waiting for me to finish my sentence. If I told him I had eaten even the tiniest speck of cyanide-laced explosives he would not only think of me as exceptionally stupid, but he would probably put me in the hospital for observation.

It had only taken a few seconds for all of these thoughts to race through my throbbing brain, but I knew I had to choose my next words carefully. "Come to think of it, the peanut butter did taste a little off. Yeah, you are probably right sir." I could see the look of satisfaction pasted across his face, as he just nodded and continued to write.

As I trudged down the road in the dark the cold night air helped clear my head. By the time I reached the shack, I was beginning to feel somewhat better. The headache had subsided into a minor throbbing pain. I was glad to see that one of the guys had dropped off my kit next to my bed. Sitting on my bedside table was a sandwich wrapped in brown wax paper, which someone had obviously sneaked out of the mess hall for me.

The building was very quiet, with the only light coming from my bedside lamp. Parkas, pants, and various bits of kit were strung about in every bed space. I knew all the guys were either in the canteen or over at Lucy's Gasthof celebrating the end of a hard week in the field and the start of a much-needed weekend off. It didn't take me long to strip away the damp, smelly field clothes I had worn all week. After popping down the 222 tablets the doc had given me, I just stood gratefully under the shower head, letting the steam and hot water soak my aching head and body. The stolen sandwich remained untouched as I crawled under the covers, thankful to be alive, thankful that my gross stupidity had not landed me in the hospital, but mostly thankful that I had the whole weekend to recover.

The balance of that last course week went by rather slowly. Although there were still some periods of instruction to cover, all of the tests and field work were done. It is quite difficult to sit there listening to a forty-minute period knowing that it is just time filler and had no real impact on the final results. This was another part of the army game I had learned during basic training. Regardless of how boring or mundane the lesson, I had become very good at faking interest.

I had seen very little of Reg Evers during the last couple of weeks. Our few brief encounters during the early weeks of the course had not gone that well. I always dreaded his lectures because I knew that at some point during the forty minutes he would try to catch me out with some obscure question. I always spent more time studying before his lessons and tried to be ready for anything he threw at me.

Each week when we received the new lecture schedule, I always took a few minutes to scan the column to see who was giving each lesson. With only three days to go, I was relieved to see that Corporal Evers had but one lesson left to teach. As always, I read and reread the material he would teach the night before.

During the lesson I sat there listening and waiting apprehensively for the inevitable question. In forty minutes he didn't ask me a single question. He barely looked in my direction. At the end of the lesson he was summarizing his final points on ammunition safety, when he said something which caught me completely off guard. "Remember, gentlemen, the best way to ensure positive safety when working around any type of explosive is to be both careful and thorough in everything you do. It took a fair amount of time to blow up that steel beam last week because it required a large number of separate charges to be tied together precisely and correctly. It was a success because Burke took his time and thoroughly checked everything before lighting the fuse." It took me a few moments after the lesson ended for reality to sink in. He had actually paid me a compliment!

Andy Bolski summed it up best as he nudged and whispered to me, leaving the classroom. "Will wonders never cease?"

On the last morning of the course we all stood around the outside smoking area waiting for our names to be called. The only thing left to do was sign our course reports. I was quite sure I had passed, but to crack the top five students and stay in pioneer platoon, I would have to do a great deal better than a mere pass.

I scanned the platoon commander's face, trying to read his thoughts, as he passed the all-important form across the desk. Normally he was a relatively friendly officer who always gave you that reserved, business-like "hello" whenever you dealt with him. This morning he was much more talkative than normal. He went on at length asking about how I was feeling after last week's incident. I had not been aware that he even knew what had happened, but I told him I was feeling fine and that seemed to satisfy his curiosity. All this time the report was right there in front of me, and although I was very anxious to read it, he continued to talk away about all manner of things. As quickly as he had started this casual conversation, he stopped and almost instantly became the business-like officer once again. "Right, read this slowly and carefully," he said, jabbing his finger on the form. I fully intended to read each and every line, but my first instinct was to go immediately to two very small blocks, halfway down the right side of the form. It took just a second to find them:

> Course Standing: "First"
> Course Grade: "A"

. . .

That afternoon we busied ourselves out in the back compound cleaning up all the remaining tools and equipment from the course. I sat there atop a wooden crate, carefully applying a fine sheen of oil to one of the many shovels we had used. For the first time in a long time I was very happy with myself. Not only had I passed, but I'd come first! Now even that arrogant twit, Corporal Evers, would have to admit he had been wrong about me. My mean spirited thoughts were suddenly interrupted by a tap on the shoulder. I was momentarily startled, as I swung around to find Reg Evers standing right above me, looking down. "Well done, Stoney. I never doubted you could do it. This is for you, but don't open them until you get back to the shack." Without another word he thrust a brown paper bag containing six cans of beer toward me and walked away.

As I stood there open-mouthed, Andy Bolski leaned over and slapped me on the back. "Two compliments in one week. He must be getting soft," was all he said. I was more than a little confused and the contents of the bag did nothing to solve the mystery.

Seeing my dilemma, the platoon store man, Lance Corporal Green, started to laugh uncontrollably. "You really don't get it, do you Burke?"

"Get what?" was all I could think to say.

"Evers and Sergeant Stoke had a bet on since day one of the course." Seeing my continued confusion, he went on with the story. "They bet a case of beer on who would top the course. Stoke picked Bolski and your buddy Reg picked you to win."

He could see I was not buying it, as I just stood there shaking my head in denial. "No way," I finally said. "How can that be? The bastard has been picking on me since day one."

"Simple," he went on. He kept at you so you would work harder." At last the light went on.

"That son of a bitch has been on my back since the beginning just to win a bet!"

Chapter 5

Is There Any Such Thing as a Dumb Question?

It took a few minutes to register, as I reached over to slam my hand down on the alarm clock, in a vain effort to turn off the incessant ringing noise. The shack was completely dark, but I could see the luminous face on my clock through half-opened eyes. It was 3:30 a.m. "What the hell is wrong with this damn clock?" I muttered to myself, as I continued to fumble for the off switch. The overhead light suddenly came on. *That's just great,* I thought to myself. *Now my bloody alarm clock has woken up the entire building!*

I was still in a state of semi-consciousness when someone shouted at me from across the room. "Come on, Burke, get your ass out of bed!" Slowly the haze lifted as I sat half up and realized that the noise was not emanating from my clock. The sound of sirens filled the air. All around me lights were going on and people were jumping out of bed. Some, like me, were just putting their feet on the floor, while others were already half dressed. Another voice startled me into full consciousness. "Get a move on Burke! What the hell you waiting for, an engraved invitation?" It had taken a few minutes, but finally the little light in my brain went on. We were having a "bug-out."

A bug-out was the slang term we used for these frequent recall exercises. It was assumed that someday the Russians would no doubt attack all across Western Europe. From their positions in East Germany, it would not take very long to reach us in this these forward NATO positions in the Ruhr Valley. The experts had long predicted that we would have approximately twelve hours to move into a defensive position and prepare for what was sure to be a massive aerial and artillery bombardment, followed immediately by wave upon wave of tanks and ground-mounted infantry. To prepare for such an onslaught we carried out these exercises aimed at getting us and all our equipment and ammunition into position and ready to fight as quickly as humanly possible.

During the initial workup training in Canada, we had received numerous lectures on this important subject and this continued throughout our time in

Germany. The emphasis was always on what the Warsaw Pact was expected to do and what NATO would do to counter the threat. According to the experts our job was to "hold" the enemy until such time as reinforcements could arrive from Great Britain and North America. Even the most optimistic estimates put this "holding" action at ninety-six hours. Even though my friends and I were all just young, dumb privates, we would often get into to some rather heated discussions about these tactical theories we were being taught. Just in tanks alone, it was no secret that the Warsaw Pact outnumbered NATO by a ratio of ten to one. When it came to manpower, we were told that the combined numbers of German, Belgium, British, American, and Canadian forces in Europe was about 100,000 men. Although the actual number was unknown, the most conservative estimates for Warsaw Pact front-line soldiers was put at over half a million. We may have been complete novices when it came to tactics, but even we understood that it would be virtually impossible for such a relatively small NATO force to remain in a static position and hold such a massive juggernaut at bay for four days.

It always amazed me that whenever we sat through one of these lectures on the tactical situation, no one ever asked the hard questions. From the day I had first learned I was going to Germany, I had done a fair amount of reading on this crucial subject. Many times I had the urge to stick up my hand and just ask, but when I looked around the room and saw all those agreeing nods from people I knew to be more intelligent than me, I just sat there and said nothing.

It would take me all of thirteen years to finally get an answer to this puzzling question. I was sitting with twenty other warrant officers on the infantry sergeant major's course, in Gagetown, New Brunswick, listening intently as our guest lecturer from the directorate of strategic studies talked about the very subject that had fascinated me for so long. As I strained to take in everything he said, I couldn't help but feel the irony in his words. It may have been the dawn of the 1980s, but the basic principle of the "holding battle" was still the accepted doctrine.

When he finally began to sum up, I anxiously waited for him to ask for questions. When he did, I flung my hand in the air immediately. It was readily apparent from his presentation that this man knew what he was talking about. I was keenly aware that there was a good reason why he was up there on stage talking and I was the sitting close to the back of the room, listening. After getting to my feet, I cleared my throat nervously. "As you are no doubt well aware sir, the Canadian brigade in Germany is fully mechanized, and the same holds true for practically all the NATO forces in Western Europe." Watching him as I spoke, I could see him smile and nod, as if he knew what was coming next. "We were all taught very early on that mechanization gives us a speedy and flexible response to any enemy threat. If all that is true, why would we give it up and dig into a static defensive position?" From my position near the back of the room, I could see a few heads turn to see the source of the question. A couple of heads nodded in agreement, but most just looked a bit confused. My first instinct was to keep talking, in an effort to try and qualify my question, but instead I just stood silently waiting for his response. He walked back and forth for a few moments, as if debating what to say. Finally he spoke.

"Politics," was his one word reply. A low buzz filled the room as people tried to decipher what he meant. I could see he was enjoying the moment, as he continued to silently survey the room. When the buzz finally stopped, he spoke. "I assume you are all aware of what happened on the eastern front in the summer of 1941? If you are not familiar with the German invasion plan known as *Operation Barbarossa*, I strongly suggest you read up on it." Again he paused for just a moment. "When the German army swept across the Russian border, the Red Army's response was to withdraw. As they retreated east they literally burned, bulldozed, and flattened everything left behind. What the Russians achieved was time and space. Their continual withdrawal to the east forced the Germans to stretch their resources and burn their fuel as they went even deeper into Russia without making any significant enemy contact. When the Russian winter finally struck, the German supply lines were already stretched over thousands of miles across eastern Europe and into Russia." He paused for just a moment to let this sink in. "What has that got to do with us today?" he asked rhetorically. By then I had sat back down, but he pointed in my general direction and carried on. "Your question is valid one, and you're right. By dismounting and fighting from a static position, we are going against the very principles of 'mobility' and 'flexibility,' but that is exactly what we are going to do." Again he paused for effect. "The smart thing to do would be to fight a retrograde battle. Hit the enemy quick and hard and as soon as they get ready for a full blown counter attack, back off and keeping running west. You slow down their momentum by destroying every road and bridge you cross. What have you achieved?" he asked. "NATO would achieve time and space for reinforcements to arrive, while the enemy's resources would be stretched to the limit. Their supply lines would be stretched over hundreds, perhaps thousands of miles, and their advancing columns would remain very vulnerable to air attack." Again he took a long pause to let everything sink in.

"So, getting back to the original question of why not do it that way, the answer, as I said in the beginning, is simple: politics, or more specifically European politics. To fight this type of battle would mean giving up all of West Germany, along with a great deal of territory in Holland, Belgium, and France. The governments of Western Europe are obviously not to keen on the idea of just handing over their territory."

Seeing the sobering effect his words had on the group, he asked if there were any more questions. When none were forthcoming, he again walked to the front of the stage, surveying the audience. "Gentlemen, I want to make this point perfectly clear. I consider this a privileged platform, and what I've said to you is a personal opinion only. Hopefully we will never have to find out which strategy is right. Remember also that NATO is not just blindly standing by, hoping that this strategy of forward defence will work. I know that all of you are aware of the REFORGER exercises that are held in Germany during the fall of each year. What some of you may not know is that this exercise is not held simply to test the NATO forces already on the ground, but, more importantly, to test the rapid deployment of troops and equipment from the U.S. and Great Britain. Hence, the term REFORGER has a simple mnemonic meaning — Reinforcements to Germany."

I learned a great deal on that course in Gagetown, all those years ago, but probably the most valuable lesson I took away from there was the understanding that when you don't know the answer to something, there is no such thing as a stupid question. My only regret was not asking a decade earlier.

• • •

The call to "bug out" could come at any time, day or night. Our first indication of an alert would be the high-pitched wail emanating from the sirens scattered about the base. Everyone moved with a sense of urgency, because we never knew if this was the real thing or just another in a never ending series of exercises. The first blare of the sirens sent the five company duty drivers scrambling to their respective trucks. Each driver had a pre-designated route through the countryside, with the task of picking up all the married men from their homes and returning them to camp.

Now that I was fully awake, it took me less than fifteen minutes to throw on my uniform, grab my field kit, and head out the door. The first order of business was to get to the weapon stores and pick up my rifle. When I arrived at pioneer stores, the rest of the "Bastard Section" was already there. Sergeant Stokes had hung this dubious title on the five of us in the platoon who were single and living in the quarters. During any alert exercise, speed was of the essence, which meant that the five members of the Bastard Section were right there, ready to start work almost as soon as the siren sounded. The majority of the men in the platoon were married, and would take at least an hour to get into camp.

One of the most important jobs that pioneers had on one of these alert exercises was to wire the entire headquarters building for demolition. The destruction of all the material that could not be moved when we evacuated the base was a high-priority task, and therefore could not wait until the more senior, mostly married members of the platoon arrived. Barely thirty minutes had elapsed since the sirens had gone off, but already the Bastard Section was well into the job of preparing the HQ for destruction. Of course, by then we knew that it was just a mock exercise and not the start of the Third World War, but, regardless of whether the threat was real or a drill, everything was done as realistically as possible.

The normally busy headquarters building was practically deserted as I moved down the long centre hallway, carefully stringing out the electrical cable. Johnny Paquett was the most senior, and therefore in charge of our little group, at least until one of the married corporals arrived to take command of this important task. As I continued down the hall, Johnny would splice another wire into the main line and feed it into the three main target areas. The operations, intelligence, and colonel's offices all contained large, immovable safes to secure any number of secret documents, all of which must be destroyed.

When one of the corporals finally did arrive, we were already in the final stages of preparation. Everything up to this point had been done exactly as if the situation were real and the Russians were right there knocking on the front door. Realism or not, it was obvious that the commanding officer would not take kindly to having his office destroyed, so at this point all of the explosives and detonators were replaced with practice charges. A small electrical squib was used to replace the detonator and a small, plastic cylinder containing gunpowder was used to simulate the explosive charge. Johnny had the job of carefully connecting the squib to the electric cable. Once he had finished each connection, I followed along, inserting the squib into the gunpowder charge and attaching it to the combination dial on the safe. With everything in place, we headed to the other end of the building and attached the cable to the electric exploder. With a nod from the corporal, Johnny simply pushed down on the plunger and fired the charges. Instantly the air was filled with the noise of five gunpowder charges detonating simultaneously. We had taken care to open every office window, which allowed the plume of smoke from each explosion to dissipate quickly.

All that was left to do was retrieve all of the electric cable and move on to our next critical job. Johnny and I were both smiling with the satisfaction of a job well done, as we reeled in the wire. Our smiles quickly disappeared as we entered the CO's office and saw what had happened. "Oh shit," was all I could think to say, as we both looked down at the damage we had caused. The gunpowder charge had obviously fallen off the door of the safe and onto the floor. What we were staring at was a rather large, smouldering hole that had been blown straight through the CO's carpet. When I called the corporal down to survey the damage, I assumed he would be upset and ream me out for not being more careful. His reaction was quite unexpected. He began to laugh uncontrollably, as if this were the funniest thing he had ever seen.

"Well, Burke," he finally said, slapping me on the back, "they wanted these exercises to be realistic and you certainly gave them that." As we hurried out of the building to tackle our next job, all I could hope for was that the colonel's attitude to me destroying his carpet would be just as forgiving as the corporal's.

Our next critical task was the same kind of simulated demolition we had just finished in the HQ, only this one would be on a much grander scale. It was getting on toward the first light of dawn, as we hastily threw all of the equipment into the back of our armoured personnel carrier (APC) and drove out of the base, heading north.

Our APC trundled along at its maximum speed of twenty-four miles per hour. The steel-and-rubber-padded tracks allowed the vehicle to deal with practically any type of terrain. It was designed to do things and go places a wheeled vehicle could never go. Regardless of whether the ground was covered in deep snow or swampy mud, this vehicle could handle it with relative ease. With the front trim vane extended to form a bow and the bilge pumps turned on, it could even traverse a wide river with currents of up to eleven feet per second. Hard surface roads presented absolutely no problem for this vehicle, but the steel and rubber track striking the pavement made for one bumpy and uncomfortable ride for anyone sitting in the back. The battalion had taken delivery of these new APCs in early 1966, and although at first there were some complaints about the rough ride, we all quickly realized that this was infinitely better that walking.

The early morning air was cold and refreshing as Johnny Paquett and I stood up in the open cargo hatch and hung onto the tie-down straps. The vibrations emanating from the floor of the APC was deadened somewhat, as our vehicle swung off the hard asphalt road onto the softer dirt track leading to our next destination.

Some five hundred yards in, the gravel and dirt road came to an abrupt end at the front gate of the brigade ammunition depot. The area consisted of a huge rectangle, roughly 440 yards long and 110 yards wide. An electrified fence surrounded the entire enclosure. Two men with loaded weapons maintained a constant patrol on the narrow dirt path around the outside of the fence. The centre of the enclosure contained three rows of Quonset huts. All of these nondescript-looking structures were built very low to the ground and were covered in about three feet of earth. Each building was spaced about thirty feet apart, with a thick cement blast wall shielding it on both sides. Huge flood lights, capable of turning night into day, towered above each corner of the compound. All of these precautions were necessary to protect the vast quantities of anti-tank rockets, missiles, mortar bombs, artillery and tank shells, plastic explosive, and small arms ammunition contained inside.

While we had been busy going through the mock destruction of the headquarters back in Fort York, the quartermaster for each company had been here at the ammo depot, busily loading each of his trucks with everything his company would need to fight the impending battle. Even after the last truck left fully loaded, there still remained many thousands of rounds which could not be taken. Our job was simple: wire the whole place with explosives and destroy everything that remained. Of course, because this was still only an exercise we would go through most of the same drills we had used earlier that morning, with one major exception. This was, after all, a munitions storage area containing countless rounds of live ammunitions and all manner of high explosive warheads. Not even something as innocuous as an electric squib could be used, and certainly not any device containing gunpowder. All we could do was go through the steps of laying out the electrical cable.

As luck would have it, just as we were reeling out the last spool of wire, the word came over the radio: "End exercise — all stations are to stand down and return to base." Johnny and I dropped our tools and headed for the compound entrance, happy that we could kick back and relax. Thankfully, our driver, Donny Gallant, had earlier fired up the Coleman stove and had a billycan full of hot steaming coffee waiting for us. After this much-needed break, the entire crew headed back into the compound. The whole area was a buzz of activity, as each of the company quartermasters returned to offload his ammo, and we went about the tedious job of retrieving all of the electrical cable.

The sun was already high in the sky as we headed back up the road. I was feeling pretty good about how well things had gone, when suddenly I remembered the CO's carpet. I decided that the best thing to do was try putting it out of my mind. No one had mentioned it since early morning and I was not about to bring it up.

Our young platoon commander called me in to his office later that day. Sergeant Stoke had warned me that it was about the burnt carpet, so I was a little nervous as I snapped to attention in front of his desk. I need not have worried. Apparently the colonel had been more upset by the lingering odour of gunpowder in his office than he was about the rug, but once our young officer explained the CO just shrugged it off as the price you pay for realistic training.

Although we continued to do these exercise alerts on a regular basis over the next few years, I was warned to steer completely clear of the CO's office.

Chapter 6

Soaring with the Eagles in Sennelager

By early April, the long winter was beginning to lose its grip. Our first winter in Northern Germany had been somewhat of a surprise to most of us. Throughout those first two months of 1966 we awoke almost every morning to steady diet of rain and sleet. The sky remained a constant colour of grey slate. On the rare occasions when the sun managed to briefly peek through the clouds, the guys would point in mock amazement at that shiny bright light in the sky. Although it did snow periodically, it was quickly washed away by the unrelenting rain. Given a choice, I have no doubt most would have opted for a good Canadian winter.

The warmer temperatures not only heralded the arrival of spring, but also the start of the exercise season. From the beginning of May right through to late fall, we would spend the vast majority of our time in the field.

Before we could depart on the first of many field exercises, the all-important battle fitness test (BFT) must be completed by every man in the battalion. The test itself was not particularly difficult if you were properly prepared for it. Naturally, you could not just sit around for twelve months doing nothing physical and then suddenly don all your kit and run ten miles. This would be a receipt for disaster. We started many weeks earlier with marches of increasing distances every other day. By the time the actual test date arrived, we had probably walked and ran a total of one hundred miles. Although we all hated these work ups, we knew them to be necessary — but that didn't stop us from complaining. As we often said: "Practicing to route march by running five miles was a little like practicing for a punch in the mouth."

Although this test was supposed to be an annual event, no one in the brigade had done it in over eighteen months. Shortly before we arrived in Germany, one of the platoon commanders had taken his men for a route march in preparation for the test. Apparently, as they approached the front gate on the way back the young officer felt quite ill and began to throw up. Rather than let his men see him vomit, he tried to swallow it back down. Just after entering the front gate, he collapsed. Before anyone could help, he had choked to death on his own vomit. All route marches had been suspended while the investigation was going on, but once it was determined that this was just a tragic accident, testing recommenced.

The battle fitness test consisted of a ten-mile march with full equipment and rucksack. Immediately after the march, we would be required to scale a six-foot wall, jump a ten-foot ditch, and carry a man, with his full kit, a distance of two hundred yards. This wall and ditch may not sound like much, but at the end of a ten-mile march the feet tended to be blistered and sore. Landing flat footed on the other side of these obstacles was a painful, bone jarring experience. Once all of that was out of the way, we went straight to the rifle range. To successfully complete the final phase of the test we were required to fire four out of five rounds into the bull's eye of a small target.

It had always struck me as rather odd that the requirement time to complete the march varied depending upon your age. All those of us who were under thirty-five years of age had a maximum of two hours to finish the march. As

Photo courtesy of the Department of National Defence.

Before the annual exercises begin each member of the battalion must first pass the battle fitness test.

most of us soon discovered, this was impossible, even at a brisk walking pace. To succeed in the allotted time we had to vary our speed between short, fast walks and long stretches of running. Soldiers over thirty five had an extra ten minutes added, and anyone over the age of forty two had no time limit whatsoever. We were always told that you had to lead from the front, so I found this particular policy extremely odd, especially considering that almost all our supervisors were in their late thirties or early forties. In time of war, was the enemy going to be considerate enough to allow our thirty-eight-year-old section commander that extra ten minutes to catch up to us before they attacked? Many of the young guys jokingly discussed how marvelous it was going to be when we reached our middle forties and could do the battle fitness test at our leisure. I am not sure exactly when it changed, but sometime in the late 1970s somebody finally saw the error of this policy and changed the time to a standard two hours and ten minutes regardless of age. It's probably just as well I didn't know the name of the person responsible for the time change because I would have surely cursed his name as I chugged down the road on my last battle fitness test, a mere week before my fifty-ninth birthday.

• • •

After a couple of weeks of working on section level drills in the Haltern training area, we had only a short reprieve back in Fort York before departing for what was certain to be the most exciting and realistic training we would ever have.

By the time summer rolled around we had done a fair number of defensive and offensive exercises, but we all knew it was just a game, and, all things considered, we were relatively safe. Until then we had only used blank ammunition in our rifles and a small, gunpowder-filled cylinder, known as a thunder flash, to simulate grenades. All of these training aids were designed to create some level of noise and smoke on the battlefield, but obviously none came close to simulating the real thing.

The British training base at Sennelager would give us that first taste of reality.

The small town of Sennelager was just a two hour drive from Fort York. At first glance, the base looked rather small and inconspicuous. If you were driving down the town's main street and not paying attention it would be quite easy to miss the entrance altogether. The administrative area of the base consisted of a group of about fifteen nondescript-looking buildings. All of the buildings were one storey structures painted in olive drag. The colour and low-slung design of the building blended in nicely with the abundance of cedar, elm, and pine trees surrounding the base.

The purpose of this base only became apparent when you passed this built up area and proceeded through the back gate to the barrier at range control.

The range road started at the back gate and continued in a huge circle around the entire perimeter of the base. The road was like a giant wheel with smaller roads feeding off each side like spokes. Each of these spokes led to a live fire range, where almost any size and calibre of weapon could be fired. Everything from a simple pistol, to an anti-tank rocket, to a 105 millimetre artillery shell could all be fired from different ranges simultaneously.

The various types of ranges were spread out along this circular range road with each facing into the middle of the circle. Regardless of what range was firing all the expended ammunition ended up in this one common impact area, in the centre of the circle. Although this was certainly a brilliant concept, what made this particular range unique was the fact that it was one of the very few places in all of Europe where you could actually conduct a platoon, company, or even a battalion attack using live ammunition.

Pioneer platoon, along with an advance party of about fifty men, arrived in Sennelager three days before the battalion. Although there were many great reasons to be in pioneers, this job was not one of them. It seems that someone had long ago decided that the task of setting up an entire tented camp was best suited to our type of expertise. Whenever a field exercise required a temporary camp to be set up, we would be the ones to do it. Pioneers would arrive well in advance of the main body of troops and erect all the necessary canvas for every-thing from sleeping areas to kitchens and canteens. That first day we erected line upon line of bell tents. As the name would indicate, the tent was a circular, bell-like structure, designed to sleep up to six men. More than one hundred of these tents would be needed to house the entire battalion. The tent itself was relatively quick and easy to erect and could have been done in less than one day, but this being the army, it took us a day and a half to complete the task. This simple task was made difficult because each and every tent had to be absolutely straight and in line with all the others. To achieve this precision, the NCO in charge of the work party stood on the hood of a truck some distance away. As we positioned the centre pole of each tent, he would peer through his compass and shout at us to move left, right, back, or forward until everything was exactly in line. Once he confirmed we were correctly aligned, pegs would be driven in the ground to ensure nothing moved.

Once the sleeping tents were up, we turned our attention to the biggest structure of all. The mess hall and kitchen tent would be a massive undertaking. The entire canvas enclosure had to allow a large area for cooking while the majority of the space would be used for the up to three hundred soldiers to sit and eat at the same time. A circus tent would have been ideal, but, because the army didn't have anything quite so large, we would have to string together our own big top using upwards of thirty marquee tents.

Each piece of marquee tent is approximately twelve feet long with small, round holes spaced along each end. It was slow, tedious work, but, using nylon rope, we would have to knit together every available piece we had in order to form a roof long enough to cover the entire structure. Once all the poles were in place we positioned ten men on anchor ropes at each end and pulled the monstrous tent into the upright position. Once the canvas walls were in place, all that remained was to secure the bottom flaps with steel pickets.

The soldiers' canteen and the sergeants' mess tent were done with little fuss or bother, but our final construction job was proving to be a distinctly difficult task. The officers' mess tent was a relatively small affair, and what should have taken an hour at most ended up taking close to six hours to complete. The officer in charge of the mess had insisted that before we started construction the ground had to be leveled. After a frustrating two hours using shovels, rakes, and a leveling bubble we finally had a twenty-four foot square space, in the middle of this huge grassy field. With this task complete, we quickly erected the tent. We were all tired after a very long day and only wished to get away from this obviously insane officer, but that was not to be. Thinking we were done we were about to leave when he told us he wanted doors put on the tent. All of these army-issue tents came with a canvas door flap which could be easily buttoned up to secure the tent. He had brought two wooden doors that had been made back in Fort York.

I am sure the corporal in charge of our little work party was thinking the same thing as all of us. "This guy must be a complete idiot." Unfortunately, this person standing there with two wooden doors was an officer, so our thoughts were best kept to ourselves. "You see, sir, these doors are made of heavy wood," he went on in a careful but condescending tone. "There is no way we can hang these on something as flimsy as canvas."

"I understand that corporal, so I brought along some two-by-four planks and hinges you can use to build a door frame." I'm sure the poor corporal was just choking back the urge to say something, anything, to this officer, but being an experienced professional he said nothing. After a few moments of staring in disbelief he just turned to face our little group, rolled his eyes, and told us to get to work. The young officer seemed completely oblivious to our muttering as we set about our difficult task. Unbelievably, after an hour of measuring, fitting, adjusting, and refitting we managed to create something that not only looked good, but actually worked!

Again we started to pack up and leave, when once again we were stopped in our tracks by another ludicrous request. I remember thinking earlier that leveling the ground inside a tent was a rather strange thing to do. I am sure if I hadn't been so tired I would have thought it funny as we pulled roll after roll of broadloom from the truck and began laying wall-to-wall carpet throughout the entire tent.

Our tent city was situated just outside the back gate of the main camp and within walking distance of the shower point. That night in the canteen, our little group of labourers sat crowded around a table sipping on cold beer and joking about the events of the day. Our collective mood had improved a great deal by a better-than-average supper followed by a hot shower. We were happily aware that the job of construction was over and we had about ten hours to relax and sleep before the real field training would begin. My suggestion that perhaps our canteen would look much better with some nice carpeting was met with mock ridicule and a couple of empty cans being thrown in my direction. Everyone seemed to be fighting off some much-needed sleep, and by nine o'clock the battle was lost. We all headed off into the darkness to find our tent and burrow down deep in our sleeping bags. We had already been warned that the next three weeks were going to bring some intensely realistic training.

• • •

It is one thing to simply stand in a static location and fire live ammo at a target, but it is quite something else to be running forward, with forty or fifty men on either side of you, all firing live rounds. As the line moves forward and the terrain becomes rougher, each man has to deal with various types of obstacles in his path. To add to the difficulty, each man has to stop every few paces to take aimed shots. That nice, straight line quickly becomes uneven and somewhat disorganized. Before you know it there are people in front and others lagging behind. Still, the momentum of the attack carries forward. While all this is going on, there is another group, off on one of the flanks, firing belts of live machinegun rounds onto the objective. As we continue our charge forward, the machinegun bullets pepper the entire area in front of us. The final piece of realism was provided by the engineers setting off one pound explosive charges to simulate an incoming artillery barrage. From start to finish, the whole experience was one huge adrenaline rush.

As we raced forward, the whole scene was absolute bedlam. The sounds of our rifle fire mixed with the constant rattle of machinegun rounds coming from our flank all added to the organized chaos. A steady stream of explosions ripped through the area, sending plumes of black smoke high in the air. Through all of this noise we strained to hear our section commander screaming constant orders. Once we had overrun the objective and consolidated on the other side, we literally collapsed into a firing position, breathlessly facing straight ahead and waiting for our next command. The bedlam was replaced by almost total quiet. Having to no longer shout over the noise of explosions, even the section commander's voice was low and restrained. We lay there struggling to catch our breath while we quickly checked our ammo and weapons to make sure all was in order, knowing we had only minutes before we would be ordered forward into the next attack.

Photo courtesy of the Department of National Defence.

Crawling through barbwire while under fire.

Photo courtesy of the Department of National Defence.

A soldier lays in wait for the final attack. Note the smoke grenade ready to be thrown to cover the advance.

Photo courtesy of the Department of National Defence.

Firing through the smoke and haze during the final phase of an attack.

The breakneck pace of live fire training continued unabated throughout the first week. Reveille was at five o'clock, followed by a hasty breakfast of lukewarm coffee and lumpy porridge. By six o'clock we were all were already jammed tightly in the back of the truck and heading down the ring road for yet another exhausting day of training. The first six days and nights were spent on the range with supper being delivered just before last light.

During the day, practically everything was done at the double and time just seemed to fly by. Once the sun went down, everything slowed to a crawl. All the firing was still live, but great care had to be taken to ensure everyone was in the right place before firing could commence. By the time we actually started our eyes had adjusted to the lack of artificial light but only a few tentative paces into the attack and we were soon blinded as the night sky erupted with flares and the flash of explosives. For a brief moment, everything before us was brightly illuminated and then the flares would fizzle out, plunging us once again into total darkness. Under ordinary circumstances, the smart thing to do would be to simply stop and wait for our eyes to adjust. When I and everyone around me are carrying loaded weapons, stopping is definitely not a safe option. All around me in the blackness I could hear the sound of curses as we all stumbled forward, straining to see. Our section commander spewed out a steady stream of profanity as he tried to keep everyone in line and moving forward.

Photo courtesy of the Department of National Defence.

Flares and tracer ammunition fill the air during a night attack.

Even after we had reached our objective and consolidated our position, it still took more than ten minutes to check all our ammo and equipment. Before starting, the corporal had numbered us all as a means of keeping track of everyone in the dark. Just as we got ready to continue the advance, the corporal shouted for a count. After two unsuccessful attempts and a great deal more cursing, number five still had not responded.

Another fifteen minutes elapsed as we lay there waiting for the corporal to retrace our steps. Everyone was a little apprehensive as time ticked by without any sign of the missing soldier. Although nobody said it, we all knew that there was always the possibility he was laying back there somewhere in a ditch. With the deafening noise and lack of light, it would not have been difficult for someone to be shot and lay there unnoticed and bleeding in the dark. Finally the corporal came stumbling out of the blackness, and without so much as a word on the whereabouts of number five he ordered us to move forward. It wasn't until much later that night that I found out what had happened.

Donny Tanner turned out to be the elusive number five. As we boarded the truck for the return trip to the main camp, Donny sat in the back corner bench gingerly holding his leg. Apparently, just after we started forward, Donny had tumbled forward over a tree root and landed awkwardly on some rocks. Thinking he had broken his leg, he decided to simply crawl back to the start line and get some help. After looking at it, the medic quickly determined that it was only a sprained ankle. I could see that Donny was in a good deal of pain as he related the story.

"Well, at least it's not broken," I said when he finished.

"It might have been better if it was broken," Donny said with a grimace. "Maybe the corporal would have been a little more sympathetic." It wasn't so funny then, but later when Donny repeated the story even he couldn't keep from laughing. "You should have seen the look on the corporal's face when he finally found me. At first he seemed relieved that I was not dead somewhere. Even when he thought it was broken he still seemed more concerned than upset. But then when he realized it was only a sprain he just went nuts. 'Why you little bastard,' he screamed. 'You're telling me I walked all the way back here and all you did was twist your ankle? Next time you waste my time, you little prick, you better be either dead or unconscious when I find you!'" Donny couldn't stop laughing. "Can you believe it?" he roared. "I'm the one that's injured and I end up apologizing to this bastard for not being dead!"

• • •

Those first few days were a non-stop series of live-fire exercises. By the time we got back to the tent camp, cleaned our weapons, and had a shower to scrub away the layers of camouflage paint, dirt, and sweat it was closing in on midnight. There was little or no talk as we all went about the mundane routine of cleaning up. All we wanted to do was get into that sleeping bag and sink into exhausted sleep. We all knew that we had about five hours before the new day would begin with the duty corporal storming through the tent lines to rouse us from our slumber.

On the afternoon of the sixth day, we were all anxiously waiting for the company quartermaster to arrive with lunch. I assumed it would be some sort of mystery meat, potatoes, and the ever-present peas and carrots, but I was only partially right.

During basic training in the field, we had been forced to always use our mess tins for every meal. Like most, I truly hated using these metal plates because they were awkward to use and difficult to clean. Invariably, the wash water brought out by the quartermaster was lukewarm at best. Everything eaten from the mess tins took on a greasy, metallic taste. Like most of the guys I only hoped that whatever was brought out would be something that could be put between two slices of bread. That morning had been another hasty breakfast followed by an exhausting series of drills on the range, so any type of food would be welcome regardless of the taste.

The lunchtime meal that day proved to be a bit of a challenge, but with a little care and effort I was able to get the Irish stew and mash potato sandwich into me with barely a drop finding the front of my shirt.

The trick was to first ensure you spread the mash potatoes evenly on the bottom slice. After tipping the ladle to drain off the excess gravy you must carefully spread the stew on top of the potatoes. Before the liquid can seep through the layer of mash potato, you must quickly, but gently, place the top slice of bread into position. Any aggressive force on the bread would cause the entire contents of the sandwich to ooze out on all sides. The last step of actually eating this delectable meal must be done in all haste, before the semi-liquid middle soaks through everything and your masterpiece has time to disintegrate into a mushy mess right there in your hands.

Just as I was considering whether or not to ask for seconds, the company commander came driving up. Those people still eating tried to shield their food as the dust cloud kicked up by his jeep slowly enveloped us all. As soon as he alighted from the jeep, we were given the order to fall-in. "Right, gents," he started off briskly. "Your NCOs tell me that you have been doing a fine job and working hard." Until then, we had all been listening unenthusiastically, but his next words caused an instant change in everyone's mood. "I know it has been a long week and you are all tired, so I have decided to cancel tonight's exercise. Get a good night's sleep and we'll start fresh in the morning."

It was an almost surreal feeling as we all piled off the truck back into the main camp that evening. Gone was the sullen quiet of nights passed. We still had all the normal jobs to do, but tonight everyone was laughing and joking as each man went about the task of cleaning the grit and carbon from his weapon and scrubbing the dirt and grime from his body. By eight o'clock everything was clean and safely put away. The noise level in the tent lines had dropped significantly as many of the older guys unrolled their sleeping bags in preparation for a good night's sleep.

Like everyone else, I could feel the fatigue slowly creeping up on me. The smart thing to do would be to crawl into the sack and get some much-needed sleep, but the Bastard Section would never be accused of being particularly smart. On the return trip from the range we had already discussed what to do with this rare free night. By eight that evening we had already made the long walk through the main camp and were heading for the front gate anxious to see what the little town of Sennelager had to offer.

Jordie's Bar was right across the road from the front gate of the base, but because of its small sign and the nondescript front we almost missed it. The front door opened into a brightly lit and noise-filled barroom. With only three or four patrons in the entire bar, all of the noise was provided by a jukebox blaring away in the far corner. A middle-aged woman with a thick British accent greeted us with a smile as we took a seat at the bar. "And what can I get for you gents?" she shouted over the thumping sound of Los Bravos singing "Black is Black."

Even without asking, it was readily apparent that this gasthof catered almost exclusively to British soldiers. The entire wall behind the bar was covered in all manner of badges, unit patches, and every type of military paraphernalia imaginable.

By eleven o'clock we were on our sixth or seventh round of beers. It may have been a Brit bar, but the draught was definitely German, with that distinct amber colour and rich full flavour.

Once the bar lady found out we were Canadian, she turned down the music and began to talk non-stop. She had a cousin in Halifax and perhaps we knew her? I tried explaining that there were about a thousand miles and perhaps ten million people separating London, Ontario, from Halifax, Nova Scotia, but I don't think she really heard. "London!" She said excitedly. "I'm from London!" She looked a little dejected and slightly confused when I told her there was a London in Ontario. Seeing the look of disbelief on her face, I found myself trying to prove that such a place did exist.

"We even have a river called the Thames running right through the city." She just laughed and waved her hand, as if to say I was talking complete rubbish. Even with all the other guys agreeing with what I said, she still appeared unconvinced. The conversation went on until the midnight closing time, but we were careful to steer clear of anything to do with geography.

My first thought the next morning was that something must be wrong. Could it be morning already? It felt like my head had literally just hit the rolled up towel I used for a pillow, when I heard the distinct sound of the duty corporal coming through the lines sticking his head through each tent flap and threatening people who didn't immediately bolt out of the sack. My journey back to reality was a swift one, as the corporal leaned over me and pulled the top flap of the sleeping bag off my face. "Well now, ain't you a fine sight," he laughed. "You have exactly five seconds to get out of that sack or you, your sleeping bag, and air mattress are all going outside, head first!" Knowing this particular sadist as I did, I had no doubt the threat was real.

Every muscle in my body may have been aching for just a little more sleep, and even the hair on my head seemed to hurt, but somehow I managed to unzip the bag and get my feet onto the cold dirt floor. The corporal seemed to be relishing my suffering. "Burke, if you want to soar with the eagles at night, you'd better be ready to strut with the roosters in the morning!" I didn't really know what he meant nor did I really care; I just wanted him to shut the hell up and leave me alone in my suffering. Fortunately for me, everyone in our little drinking group was having the same delayed reaction that morning. Unfortunately for him, Doug Gallant was still buried deep in his sleeping bag and had not moved since all the commotion began. I felt sorry for Doug, but I have to admit I was at least a little relieved that corporal had turned his sights to another victim.

Had I been paying closer attention to the training schedule, I may have chosen not to drink quite so much that night. We were already bouncing down the road in the back of a deuce and a half truck when it struck me that being hung-over was never a particularly smart move, but this morning it was down-right dumb. We were headed for a dry training area to be tested in the stripping and assembly of various types of weapons. Although this sounded like a rather innocuous morning of training, it was anything but.

In the event of a malfunction, an infantry soldier had to be able to take apart a weapon, fix the problem, and reassemble it in just seconds. If it happened at night he would have to do this by feel rather than sight. To achieve the realism of complete darkness we would be placed in a closed wooden box throughout the exercise.

The wooden boxes were painted black and were the same rough dimensions as a coffin. To complete the test, one had to lie down on his back with the weapon resting on his chest. Once you were in place the lid on the coffin was closed, plunging you into complete darkness. You could then begin stripping the weapon, taking care to lay each piece, from left to right, across your chest. Once you felt that this first task was done, you tapped on the coffin lid. The corporal would then open a small sliding door, inspect your work, and if it was correct the door was closed and you could begin the reassembly of the weapon. Only when the entire operation was completed successfully would the corporal finally remove the full lid and allow you back into the world of the living.

If simply being stuck in this coffin-like black box wasn't enough, there was one other hurdle which only served to make the experience that much worse, especially if you happened to be suffering the ill effects of alcohol.

I have no idea if it was simply random chance or the work of some sadistic engineer, but not one hundred yards from this dry training area stood the sewage treatment plant. The entire surrounding area was cloaked in a constant foul stench that seemed to permeate everything it touched. It certainly wasn't pleasant, but after being there awhile, it at least became tolerable. However, lying on the ground inside that blackened box with the lid closed was almost unbearable. Both you and the odour were trapped inside that coffin with nowhere to go.

I like to think of myself as having a strong stomach, but the combined effects of being trapped in that box, with the fetid odour and my self-inflicted alcohol abuse completely did me in. The moment I finally got out of that coffin, I made a dead run to the woods to deposit my breakfast.

For the past fourteen days we had been working non-stop to perfect these all important basic infantry skills. At last we were told that our final week in Sennelager would be spent working on our pioneer specialty.

By mid morning of our first day on the demolition range we had completed an entire series of basic charges without a single misfire or delay of any kind. Just when I thought that this day could not have been better, our store man showed up with lunch. Unlike the company quartermasters, who had over a hundred and fifty to feed each meal, our store man only had to worry about our little group of twenty five. Scotty had even brought out paper plates and cups so we could eat an actual meal, as opposed to wolfing down a hastily made mash potato sandwich.

Soon after lunch Sergeant Stoke announced that we would be doing a somewhat different type of charge. His meaning became clear when he pointed far down range at our new target.

On a small knoll, almost a mile away, sat the remains of a huge tank. The closer we got to it, the more impressive it became. It was a relatively well-preserved forty-ton Conqueror tank. It had been built by the British, but after only a few years it was taken out of service because its sheer size and weight made it too slow and cumbersome on the battlefield. It was sad to see such an imposing piece of weaponry being reduced to nothing more than a range target, but compared to most of the other tank targets out here, this one was in almost pristine condition. This tank still had most of its road wheels attached to the hull and its long, heavy gun barrel protruded straight out from its massive turret.

Only a few months had passed since I had last used explosives. Although there had been a few comments and veiled hints made about my cyanide poisoning, I had never actually told anyone the truth. Better they go on assuming I just had a weak constitution as opposed to confirming that I had been dopey enough to poison myself. I couldn't have been happier that morning when I discovered we no longer had 808 explosive. From then on we would be using the much more user-friendly C4 plastic composition explosive which still had all of the deadly attributes of an explosive charge, without any of the serious side effects.

Obviously it still could not be ingested, but unlike the poisons in 808 that could permeate the skin and cause severe headaches, C4 could be handled without wearing cumbersome gloves.

While we had been busy that morning, Sergeant Stoke had already been down range to inspect the intended target. When all of us and the equipment were in place, he wasted no time telling us what we were going to do. "Hopefully you all remember some of the theory you learned about concussion charges back on your course?" Seeing the blank looks on all our faces, he went on. "Judging by the silence, obviously not," he smiled sarcastically. "Okay, it's simple. The energy created by an explosion will always dissipate by seeking the route of least resistance." He paused long enough to look around and see that at least some of us were beginning to understand what he was getting at. "What I want to do this afternoon is prove this theory actually works by placing a charge inside this tank and sealing all the openings with sandbags. We are going to put a concussion charge inside this tank."

This was exciting stuff. The theory was still very clear to those of us who had just finished the course only a few months earlier. Normally a concussion charge would be used to destroy some form of solid structure like a building or a bunker, but obviously you won't find any such target sitting on a range waiting for destruction. We could use this tank to turn a theory into a practical application.

There wasn't much room to work inside the tank, so the two smallest guys got the job of crawling inside the crew commander's hatch. I stood atop the main gun turret and passed bundles of C4 sticks down to the guys working inside. Sergeant Stoke stood above me on the turret ring and counted each stick as it was passed inside the hatch. After a hundred pounds I felt sure we must be close to completion but still we continued stuffing the explosives down the hatch. Finally, after feeding one hundred and fifty pounds into the beast, the guys inside confirmed that there was no room left in the turret compartment. After wrapping the last bundle of sticks in explosive cord and inserting the detonator into the middle of the large explosive pile, the two men inside squeezed back out through the open turret hatch. It took another thirty minutes to jam the hatch cover down and stack all the available sandbags on top.

Donny Tanner was given the honour of lighting the ten-foot length of fuse which would give us ample time to walk the safety distance and take cover.

Before we actually heard the explosion, I could feel the earth rumble beneath my feet. In the next split second, the air was filled with a deafening roar of energy trying to escape the confines of the tank. The tank was instantly obscured by flame and smoke. We heard a distinct thud from somewhere inside the black, billowing curtain. We could still hear the sound of the explosion echoing off in the distance as the dirty cloud quickly evaporated in the atmosphere.

What had been a mammoth tank just a few minutes earlier was suddenly nothing more than a pile of bent and twisted metal. An explanation for the loud, thumping noise was not necessary, as the cause was instantly apparent.

The fifteen-ton gun and turret lay on its side smouldering about twenty feet behind what was left of the tank hull.

The next few days on the demolition range were a whirlwind of non-stop activity. By mid week we had used most of our four thousand pound allotment of explosives on every type of target imaginable. We may not have had a bridge to work on, but we did have a number of massive metal girders on which to practice our steel-cutting skills. Obviously we could not destroy any of the asphalt roads in the area, but there were numerous dirt tracks readily available to practice our route denial procedures. After first drilling a seven-foot-deep hole in the middle of the road, we then fed over a hundred pounds of C4 down into the chamber. Once the fuse was lit, we quickly retreated to a safe distance. The subsequent detonation sent rocks and debris hundreds of feet into the air. When the dust settled, we were left with a circular hole more than ten feet deep and spanning the entire width of the road. If this were the real thing, this gaping hole would certainly slow down or even stop the enemy's advance.

With only a few days remaining before the end of the exercise, our young officer called me aside at lunch to give me a new assignment. I would be working with Bravo Company, blowing blinds on the grenade range for the balance of the week. Many of the grenades we still had in use were left over from the Second World War and had become highly unreliable, with approximately one in ten failing to explode once they were thrown. My job for the next few days would be to destroy these "blind" but still very dangerous grenades right where they landed.

The first order of business was to check in with range control and pick up everything I would need to do the job. After following the sign from the main road, I arrived at the range control compound that consisted of a line of buildings and what appeared to be storage sheds. Not knowing where to report, I pulled up next to a group of German civilians that were sitting around a picnic table drinking coffee. I wanted to ask them where I could find the office, but as soon as I got close enough, their appearance stopped me in my tracks.

Of the six men sitting and standing around the table, not one was whole. Each one of them had either a wooden leg or a hook-like claw where a hand should have been. *Good God*, I thought. *Are these the guys they use to blow up defective ammunition?* I knew there was a serious element of danger associated with this job, but to have such blatant evidence of the danger standing right there in front of me was quite disconcerting.

"I am looking for the range control office." I said. I knew it was extremely rude, but I couldn't stop staring.

One of the men had a broad smile on his face, and after a moment's pause, he pointed his one good hand toward the office. "You go there." After finally drawing my eyes away, I thanked them and started toward the building. "What is it you do?" He shouted after me. He obviously knew the source of my discomfort, and once I told him what I was doing on the grenade range, his smile became a laugh as he held up his metal-hooked hand.

"Don't look so worried, these are from the war."

As I found out later, these men were all handicapped veterans of the Second World War and had been hired by the Brits because of their expertise with explosives. To this day, whenever I find myself becoming a little too complacent around explosives, I think of those men and my focus returns.

It had been little more than one year since I had actually thrown one myself, yet here I was, sitting in a concrete bunker waiting to destroy any grenades that failed to explode. Even with my limited experience, I knew that misfires were inevitable when you were dealing with the M36 grenade. The much newer M67 and V40 grenades came already assembled. All you had to do was remove it from the container, pull the pin, and throw. The problem was that we still had a large number of the Second World War vintage grenades that had to be used up first.

The M36 came in two separate pieces, each packed in beeswax and grease. Once the packing grease was removed one could then unscrew the base plug, insert the detonator, and reassemble the grenade. Then and only then was it ready to be thrown. Even the smallest speck of grease could prevent the striker lever from flying off or not allow the fuse to ignite the detonator. The cleaning problems, combined with the fact that they had been sitting in storage for over twenty years, led to an abnormally high rate of failure. I wouldn't have long to wait.

I have to admit to being more than a little nervous. The vast majority of soldiers in Bravo Company were guys I had gone through basic training with. They were all no doubt aware that I had only ever thrown two grenades myself and this was my first experience blowing blinds. My mind was in a constant loop as I kept rehashing the step-by-step procedures I would have to follow.

With a stick of C4 tucked under my arm and the detonator and fuse held carefully between my thumb and index finger I headed down range to destroy the first of many dud grenades. As I took my first tentative steps into the impact area, I could see the unexploded grenade sitting in a shallow depression some forty feet away. I made a conscious effort to look nonchalant, knowing that every set of eyes in the company were watching from a safe distance. I was somewhat relieved to be doing this alone because at least my nervous heavy breathing could not be heard.

"Hang on there, young fella. I want to see what you're doing."

"Damn," I said under my breath. I didn't have to turn around to know it was the company command.

Danny Roland was the commander of Bravo Company and a legend in the battalion. Whether in uniform or not, he always carried this big knotted shillelagh walking stick tucked under his arm. He was never averse to using his stick against anything or anybody that got in his way. On more than one occasion he had been escorted from the hockey rink after reaching over the boards to club a referee after what he deemed to be a poor call.

I could feel his warm breath on the back of my neck as I went about the business of preparing the dud for destruction. I found his close scrutiny a little odd. He had been in the army for close to twenty years and fought in Korea, so I assumed he probably knew a good deal more about explosives than me. After finding a large rock, I placed it carefully down on the far side of the grenade. I next made a small hole in the plastic explosive and gently pushed the detonator deep inside. I placed the whole charge as close to the dud as possible without actually touching it or moving it in any way.

Big Dan continued to watch my every move but said nothing.

After lighting the four foot length of fuse, we began the slow walk back behind the bunker. Almost on cue, the device exploded. After a moment's wait for the dust to settle, Major Roland and I made our way back out to check the site. All that was left was a small hole where the grenade used to be. After a cursory glance around the impact area, he smiled and walked away. "Well done," he called over his shoulder. Before I was even back at the bunker he was already yelling at his company to get back to work.

By the time the last range day rolled around, I had dealt with a total of seven dud grenades, all without incident.

That evening, after the ranges had closed for the last time, the activity level throughout camp was at a fever pitch. Everywhere you looked people were scurrying about trying to clean weapons, organize personal kit, and load trucks before darkness fell.

When I woke just after dawn the next morning I sat bolt upright. There was something unusual that morning, and it took a few minutes to register what that was. It was the silence.

Without the sound of portable radios blaring away or the duty NCO yelling threats at those still in the sack, the silence was almost eerie. The main body of the battalion had departed the evening before, leaving only pioneer platoon and a small work party to pull down the entire tent camp.

Considering that we no longer had to worry about tent alignment, wooden doors, or level floors, the camp teardown went amazingly fast. Weather conditions had remained relatively warm for the last week in Sennelager, which meant the canvas was dry and easy to fold.

By mid afternoon, the big, grassy field looked like a huge, oversized patch quilt of green and brown. Everywhere you looked there was a mixture of brown circles, squares, and rectangles where tents had once stood shielding the grass underneath from the sun's rays.

With the kitchen tent down, the cook had prepared an excellent steak dinner for our small work party on a makeshift barbeque. Before pulling down the last of the canteen tents someone had managed to scrounge a couple of cases of cold beer from the bartender. Since nearly all of the canvas was down the regulations regarding open fires had been relaxed, allowing us to build a big bonfire.

That evening was one of those perfect moments in time when all seemed right with the world. Sitting there eating a steak and sipping on a beer was certainly a good feeling but adding a roaring fire and a star filled sky made the night truly memorable.

Chapter 7
The Happy Gang

The first day back in Fort York after a prolonged field exercise always felt odd. Within an hour of working indoors, the face became red and flushed and sweat soaked the body from the artificial heat of the building. The ability to simply sit at a table to eat using a knife and fork even made the normally mundane mess hall food seem to taste better. After sleeping on the ground, with only an air mattress and poncho to keep back the dampness, even my simple metal frame bed and foam mattress felt like absolute luxury.

After a week back in camp, the big day we had all been looking forward to finally arrived. Everyone seemed to be in a better mood on the last day of the month. Even the guys who usually dragged themselves out of bed at the very last minute were already up and dressing when the duty corporal came through the shack, just after reveille. Today we would not only get our regular pay, but a good deal extra, in FOE. Field Operational Expense paid us an additional $5 for every day spent in the field. This was a new allowance that we were about to receive for the first time. It may not sound like much, but when you are only getting somewhere in the neighbourhood of $200 a month, an additional $105 for three weeks in the field is a huge windfall.

When work finished that afternoon, I headed straight for the shack for a quick shower and change of clothes. The guys and I had decided at lunchtime that we would forgo supper, opting instead to grab a bite downtown.

I felt a momentary twinge of guilt as I looked at the mess left in my bed space. My uniform sat crumpled on the bed and my muddy boots sat untouched on top of my barrack box. My common sense side told me to take the time to iron my uniform and clean the boots. I knew I couldn't do it when I got back because that would involve a certain amount of noise and lights being turned on, which would not go over very well with my older, grumpier roommates. My dumb side told me to get the hell out and have fun. All this housekeeping nonsense could wait until morning. After momentarily weighing my options, the stupidity cells in my brain won and I headed out the door.

Taxi cabs were not allowed on the base, but we were just too happy at the prospect of just getting out of camp to even care about the long walk to the front gate. The five of us were definitely in a boisterous mood as we headed up the main road. All the loud talk and horseplay came to an abrupt end as we cut through the transport compound and got within fifty-five yards of the main gate. To the casual onlooker we probably looked somewhat respectable. Cigarettes were extinguished and hands came out of pockets as we quietly made our way past the guardroom and the ever-watchful eye of the military police. The dress code for leaving camp was much more relaxed than it had been in Canada, but jeans and t-shirts were still forbidden. Aside from these obvious code violations, the duty MP could also send you back if he thought you looked untidy or scruffy. Although most of the guys presented the very picture of cleanliness and sobriety on their way out the gate, many would experience great difficulty remaining upright as they wobbled back through the front gate in the wee hours of the morning.

The city of Soest was much different from any urban centre found in North America. The first settlement had been built in the eleventh century, and many of the original buildings, roads, and fortifications were still intact. The boundary of the old inner city was easily discernable by the massive wall that circled the original fortified settlement. Outside the wall, everything was relatively new and modern. Inside the wall, the old city was a labyrinth of narrow, cobblestone streets lined with tiny wood-frame houses. The market square sat at the very heart of the ancient city, with an immense gothic cathedral dominating the entire area.

Tucked away just off the northwest corner of the market was our first destination for the night: the Salvation Army. The Sally Ann Café, as we liked to call it, was a small cafe just inside the main door, and catered mostly to the Brit and Canadian soldiers in the surrounding area. The food may not have been fancy, but it was like a small taste of home. A hot dog, fries, and a milk shake cost the equivalent of 75 cents. Regardless of how often we went in there, the same lady was always behind the counter. Elizabeth was an older, grey-haired English lady, who never failed to greet us with a smile. "What can I get you my darling?" was her standard greeting to anyone approaching the counter.

Even soldiers who had never set foot in the cafe still knew Elizabeth well for her famous Sally Ann truck, which seemed to magically appear on all field

Photo courtesy of the Department of National Defence.

The Corps of Drums give a concert in the market square in downtown Soest.

Photo courtesy of the Department of National Defence.

Members of pioneer platoon lead the battalion on parade through the city of Soest.

exercises. I had heard stories of entire convoys completely lost in the forests of West Germany. Just as they were about to lose hope of ever finding their way out of the woods, Elizabeth would appear in her big blue truck. Once you had a sandwich and a big mug of tea, she would happily give you directions back to the main road.

Once we had finished our meal, we got down to the real business of exploring the many fine gasthofs Soest had to offer, or at least those that were known to be friendly toward soldiers. Like most German cities and towns, Soest had at least two or three gasthofs on each and every block. As the guys used to say: "You couldn't swing a dead cat anywhere in downtown Soest without hitting a bar sign." There may have been fifty to sixty bars in the old city core alone, but only a select few would have anything to do with riff raff such as us. We may have been halfway around the world, but if you are a soldier dealing with civilians, certain fundamental truths remain unchanged, regardless of the location. The ten thousand soldiers and civilian dependents living and spending money in the surrounding area may have been an intricate part of the local economy, but that didn't mean the local civilians wanted any direct contact with us.

Photo courtesy of the Department of National Defence.

Elizabeth and her big blue "Sally Ann" truck would frequently appear to dispense sandwiches and tea during field exercises.

Our first destination was a short walk up the narrow cobblestone street to the Oasis Bar. While still over a block away, we could hear the intermittent sound of loud music. One second it would be muffled and the next it would reach a high pitch as the front door was momentarily opened by the constant flow of people going in and out.

The Oasis was located in a small, inconspicuous structure, sandwiched between the main train station and the bus terminal. In daylight it would be very easy to miss because of all the massive buildings surrounding it. A tacky neon sign showing a one-legged flamingo standing next to a palm tree hung above the main door. The big pink *O* on the sign had long ago burned out, leading you to believe you had reached the "asis" Bar.

As we opened the front door we were greeted by a virtual wall of noise. It took a few moments for the eyes to adjust to the dim light, as we fought our way slowly toward the bar. With absolutely no hope of finding an empty stool, the four of us only managed to eke out a tiny patch of free space at the end of the bar. It took a little time to get the attention of the waitress, but using a series of hand gestures and mouthing the word "beer," she slapped down four bottles of Becks, along with four glasses. The normal procedure in most German bars was to drink at your leisure and pay before departing. With the waitress standing there, looking impatient with her hand extended, we quickly realized that she wanted her money and she wanted it now. After handing her the unheard of amount of ten marks, she only cracked the faintest of smiles before disappearing down the bar.

After leaving the noisy confines of the Oasis, our next stop was the relative quiet of the Red Patch Club. Unlike the other bars in town, the Red Patch was a Canadian-owned-and-operated club. The first time I saw the place my initial impression was that it was a structure oddly out of place with its surroundings. The two-storey building sat at the end of a narrow cobblestone lane, just inside the old city wall. The modern look of the club's exterior was in stark contrast to the ancient church and homes that sat on either side of it.

After being wedged into a corner at the Oasis Bar, this place was a little like being in a big open barn. We could hear our own footsteps as we made our way down the floor to one of the many empty booths lining the walls. Other than a few guys playing darts in the game room, we were the only patrons in the place. This was the first time we had actually sat down all evening, so it took a few minutes of looking around, followed by a visit from the bartender, to realize that there was no table service.

Karl was not your typical-looking bartender. He had a short, wiry frame, and judging by the snow-white hair and deep creases in his face, he had to be in his mid to late sixties. Standing there in his old tweed cardigan, sipping a large glass of milk, he looked like a man who had had a hard life and deserved to be sitting at home resting in front of a fire, not standing behind a bar serving kids like us.

First impressions can often be wrong, and they certainly were in this case. Karl may have looked the grandfatherly type, but he was one of the liveliest and most energetic people I was ever to meet. Whenever I was in town, I always tried to drop by the Red Patch to have a chat. Whether there was five or fifty people there looking to be served, nothing seemed to phase or rattle him. He actually seemed to thrive on the challenge as he moved about behind the bar. I would watch him in amazement as he lined up glasses to pour draft with one hand, while filling a shot glass of whiskey with the other, and never spill a drop of either. Our conversation would continue throughout his performance, only stopping long enough for him to take another drink order.

When things were quiet, his conversation would become more serious. I would stand at the end of the bar and listen, fascinated, as he told me about his wartime experience on the Russian front. When I had asked him once if he had been afraid of the Russians, he stared for a long moment before answering. "Yes, we had some fear of the soldiers, but our biggest fear was the cold. The last winter of the war we retreated constantly and lost everything except the clothes on our backs. Many of my friends just lay down and never got up again. They froze to death in the snow." I just stood there listening. There just was nothing to say. Karl looked to be far away, but after a momentary vacant stare, he broke the silence. "Ya ya," he said, holding up yet another glass of milk. "I may have stomach ulcers, but at least I'm still alive."

One of the main attractions to the Red Patch was the price of drinks. Practically every type of drink, whether it be beer or hard liquor, was just 50 pfennigs, or roughly thirteen cents Canadian. Considering that the other guys had paid ten marks for a round at the last bar, I could hardly come back to the table having spent just two marks for four drinks. I may have gone a little overboard, but nobody complained when I put a tray of ten rye whiskey and Cokes on the table. From that day forward, whenever we went to the Red Patch, drinks were always ordered by the tray. The fact that by the time you got to the third drink on the tray you were drinking lukewarm whiskey and flat Coke didn't seem to matter. Actually, most of the time there would still be four or five drinks left untouched when we got up to leave.

Within the hour, we were once again on the move, searching for a little fun and excitement. After following the old city wall through a series of narrow and confusing lanes, we finally immerged back on the main street, in front of my favourite bar in all of Soest: the Candlelight.

I don't know if it was the place itself or perhaps the people who worked there, but there was definitely something that always kept me coming back. As bars go, it was nicer than most. It was laid out in two levels, with a long oak bar filling the entire right side of the lower area. Although this level was relatively small, the floor-to-ceiling mirror behind the bar gave you the false impression of open space. A very ornate railing flanked both sides of the six steps leading to the upper level. Fortunately, the bottom of the staircase was thickly carpeted for the odd guy who failed to negotiate the steps at closing time each night.

Almost as soon as we made it through the door, a huge roar went up from the small gang of guys sitting at a table in the far corner of the room. Whether you saw them in the canteen at camp, at the Ranch House outside the hole in the fence, or in one of the many bars downtown, there were two things you could rely upon: the five of them were always together and the five of them were never sober. What separated these guys from the pack and made them so memorable was their unending good humour. When you were around them, their jokes, pranks, and constant laughter were absolutely infectious. I don't remember all their names, but collectively we all referred to them as the "Happy Gang." Whenever I ran into them they would always insist I join in the fun. I never lasted long, because within a minute of sitting down someone would do something bordering on the insane.

Majorky would pull off his shoe, fill it with beer, and offer you a drink. Whenever Stewart got up to use the toilet, he would first throw a couple of discarded cigarette butts and drop his false teeth into his beer glass. All of these strangely bizarre steps were taken to ensure no one took a sip of his beer while he was away. As soon as he disappeared through the bathroom door, one of the guys would grab the beer in a sweeping gesture and down the entire thing, leaving only the false teeth sitting at the bottom of the glass. "He has to do a lot better than that if he expects to hang on to his beer," the culprit would say as he slapped the empty glass back down on the table.

At the time, we all thought their antics were just hilarious, albeit a little strange, but in retrospect, I believe their behaviour bordered on insanity. One thing I do know is that regardless of how odd or in poor taste their behaviour may have been, it was never hurtful toward anyone. The only one in the group I knew well was "Happiness Stewart," and on the rare occasions when I actually spoke to him alone, all I saw was a kind and good-natured soul who could not hurt a fly.

The Happy Gang finally broke up at the end of the 1960s, when each was posted to different locations in Canada. Some years later, I heard a rumour that Majorky had died while attending a course in Gagetown, New Brunswick. Apparently he had been drinking heavily at one of the bars in Oromocto, just a short walk from the front gate of Base Gagetown. At closing time he decided to walk back to his room on the base, despite the fact that it was bitterly cold and snowing. No one really knows what happened, but early the next morning his body was found in a shallow drainage ditch just off the side of the road. He was only about two hundred yards from the front gate of camp. He had died of exposure.

In the mid 1990s, I heard through the military grapevine that Happiness Stewart had been killed in a car accident somewhere in Nova Scotia. Sometime later, while watching a CBC news show, I was stunned to hear that his death had not been an accident, but rather his wife had allegedly murdered him by running him down with her car.

It was well past eleven o'clock when the Happy Gang finally staggered out of the Candlelight. Before leaving they had graciously invited us to join them for a bite to eat next door at Dicka Willy's Restaurant. It had been about six hours since we had left the Sally Ann, and we were more than a little hungry. We all knew from experience that eating with these guys could be hazardous to your health. If they weren't throwing food around, they were stuffing everything from pork chops to french fries into their pockets in case a snack was needed on the taxi ride home.

The first time I was in there and witnessed these guys start a food fight, I wondered why Kurt, the owner of the restaurant, would put up with these lunatics hurling food around his dining room. It took only one conversation with Kurt to realize that he was more than a little bit bent himself.

Considering the many times I went to Dicka Willy's, I don't ever remember seeing Kurt sober. He would stand behind the bar drinking shot after shot of schnapps and chasing each one down with a draft beer. On the rare occasion when I actually spoke to Kurt, the only subject other than alcohol that seemed to interest him was soccer. To say he was a fan would be a gross understatement. When it came to European football, Kurt was a complete fanatic.

When England and Germany played in the World Cup final in 1966, Kurt invited everyone to come and watch. He had even rented a colour television for the big event. Having never seen a colour TV before, I got there early enough to get a good seat near the front of the restaurant.

The place was packed with equal amounts of Germans and Canadians, all drinking beer and having a good time watching the game. Naturally, all the Canadians in the bar were cheering for England. At first this only made for some good-natured banter between the two groups, but as the game went on, with England ahead, Kurt began to curse and throw things at the TV set. When the game finally ended in an English victory, all of the Germans sat sullen and quiet in their seats while our little group of Canadians jumped around, hooting and hollering. Judging by the look of anger on Kurt's face, I have no doubt that given half a chance he would have happily killed us all. Without a word, he walked out from behind the bar, picked the TV off the table, and threw it against the wall. Once it landed on the floor, he began to kick and stomp the shattered remains with both feet. We all just stood there, in stunned disbelief as he spit out an unending string of German curse words while continuing to assault this very expensive colour television. By the time he stopped and leaned against the wall, out of breath, bits of glass tube and plastic knobs littered the entire floor.

It looked like the tirade was finally over, when someone, probably a Canadian, began applauding and whistling. "Way to go Kurt, you definitely showed that mother-fuckin' TV!"

Any hope of restraint was lost, as Kurt began yelling and screaming. We couldn't understand the words, but the meaning was very clear — Canadians were no longer welcome in his restaurant.

Considering we were his biggest source of income, I am sure he lost a good deal of money. After a couple of weeks of stubbornness, he finally allowed us back in with the clear understanding that that any discussion about soccer was strictly forbidden.

There was a noise bylaw in Soest that required most bars in the inner city to close at one o'clock each night. As we left the restaurant and turned back on to the main road, the foot traffic was steadily increasing as people began to pour out of the bars and onto the street. Small knots of Germans civilians, along with Canadians, Belgian, and French soldiers filled the sidewalks and overflowed into the middle of the road. Some were visibly upset and banging on the bar door, demanding to be let back in. Most were just standing around trying to decide what to do next. Fortunately, our little group knew exactly where we wanted to go, as we all piled into a cab for the short ride to the edge of town.

The Copa Cabana bar sat isolated in a large open field at the very eastern edge of town. Even though the Copa had only opened for business at eleven that night, the place was already packed when we got there. For all those drunks still capable of standing even partially upright, this was the only game left in town. Everywhere you looked people were stumbling and crawling out of taxi cabs. As we made our way through the crush of bodies blocking the front door, it was every man for himself. When I finally managed to get inside and work my way toward the bar, it still took a few minutes of searching to find the remnants of our little group.

As I looked around the hundred or so people there, I don't believe there was a single sober person in the entire place. I couldn't help but think that anyone silly enough to come here sober would surely think he had inadvertently stumbled into an insane asylum. The entire room was blanketed in a thick blue haze of cigarette smoke. The noise level was absolutely deafening, as a live band hammered out a barely recognizable version of "Proud Mary." Any attempt at conversation was quickly lost, as the noise of the guitar amplifiers drowned out everything but the loudest scream. Even ordering a beer had to be done by holding up the required number of fingers and pointing at one of the many display bottles lining the back of the bar.

Every so often the band would suddenly stop playing right in the middle of a song. We all knew that this could only mean one thing: yet another fight had broken out. As the night wore on, the fights would increase to the point where the band rarely made it through a single song, without at least one stoppage.

I could not help but notice the giant of a man sitting just down the bar from me. His leather hockey jacket told me that he was with the Royal 22nd Regiment, or as they were better known, the Van Doos. A large crest on his left sleeve denoted a set of cross rifles with his nickname stitched below. His name tag simply contained the words MR BIG. All it took was one quick glance in his direction to realize that the name on his jacket was completely redundant. The man was a monster, standing over six and a half feet tall, and an easy 250 pounds. He continually swivelled his massive head back and forth, surveying the entire room. His ruddy complexion and tight, brush-cut hair made him look all the more menacing.

Within about fifteen minutes I was actually beginning to enjoy myself. Although the music was not particularly good, at least it was a live band. Even my eyes had stopped watering as they adjusted to the curtain of smoke that filled the entire room. I thought to myself that I surely must be going deaf, because even the noise from the band seemed less intense. Conversation was still impossible, so I just stood there, beer in hand, just resting against the bar and taking in the atmosphere of the whole place.

With all the bodies in such close proximity, it took me a moment to realize that there was another hand pulling at my beer bottle. I turned around instantly and started to pull back. Our little tug of war continued, as I used my free hand to try and push the drunk backwards. I had a moment of dread when I saw my adversary's Van Doo jacket, and realized I seen this guy before. He had been sitting and talking just minutes ago with Mr. Big.

Our little seesaw battle continued until finally I managed to wrestle the beer out of his hand. He immediately lunged forward, taking a wild swing at my head, but only managed to hit my arm and send the half empty beer bottle crashing to the floor. His forward momentum sent his head straight into my chest. Acting on instinct, I instantly wrapped my left arm around him in a headlock and began pummelling him with my right fist. I may have had the momentary advantage, but the guy was strong and swinging wildly with both hands. Five or six blows landed hard against my ribs, but still I hung onto his head and tried in vain to wrestle him to the floor. Although the fight had only been going on for less than a minutes, I could already feel myself getting tired, but I was not about to loosen my grit on this madman. I could feel him slowing down as well, but just as I thought that the battle was won, I saw something out of the corner of my eye and knew immediately that I was about to die.

Striding across the floor toward us was the immense figure of Mr. Big, and he looked anything but happy. I still held my opponent in a tight headlock, as my eyes flashed left and right for any sign of help, but my friends were nowhere to be seen. As the monster loomed over both of us, I just closed my eyes knowing that one blow from his huge meaty fists would probably decapitate me.

I could feel a powerful hand grabbing at the back of my jacket. When I opened my eyes, Mr. Big had one hand on each of us, and, with seemingly no effort, he pulled us both apart. "Okay, you stop now, enough!" My opponent still seemed to have a little fight left in him, but I was just happy to still be alive and was more than willing to comply. When his friend finally calmed down, Mr. Big let us go. His friend said something to him in French that I didn't understand, but Mr. Big looked clearly annoyed as he pointed at the bar. "Your beer is right there." The guy looked at little sheepish, and he walked away without a word. The thought of demanding a new beer to replace the broken one briefly crossed my mind, but I decided to leave well enough alone.

By then my friends had magically appeared back at the bar. Someone offered me a beer but I declined. I felt more than a little tired and sore from my minor ordeal and only wanted to get out of there. I know it was childish, but I felt that getting up and leaving too soon would look like he had forced us out. I was hoping one of the guys would suggest leaving for home, but I wasn't about to bring it up.

I was trying to look nonchalant about the whole thing as I stood there pretending I was actually enjoying the band. I felt a small tap on my shoulder, and when I turned around I was once again face to face with Mr. Big. Face to face is actually a bit of a misnomer, because with his towering frame in front of me, it was more like my face to his chest. Without a word, he handed me a beer. This was the last thing I wanted, but I wasn't about to refuse this guy. I just smiled and tried to look grateful. After a friendly slap on the shoulder, which I felt throughout my upper body, he and his friend headed toward the door.

Although I was to go to the Copa many times in the next few years, I only saw Mr. Big there on one other occasion. It was perhaps six months after the fight, and he was sitting at a small table in the corner with a woman that I recognized from the Penguin Bar. He gave me a nod of acknowledgement as I passed by, but we never spoke.

It was unclear exactly why the fight started, but I believe it had something to do with some disparaging remarks made about Mr. Big's female companion by some drunks at the next table. All I heard was the sound of bottles and glasses breaking as Mr. Big's table was forcibly toppled over. No less than four guys came at him, and he flung each one aside. At one point two of these guys grabbed him from behind. With both of them hanging off his back, Mr. Big ran straight backwards and slammed them both against the wall. By the time the fight ended, four limp bodies lay strung about the floor like ragdolls. He just stood there ready and waiting for the next assault. As I watched this one-man wrecking crew, all I could think was how fortunate I had been not to have gotten on this guy's bad side.

Chapter 8
... And Miles to Go Before We Sleep

The stifling heat of August was soon replaced by the almost constant autumn rain. A good downpour once in a while would have been much more preferable to the steady, unending drizzle we experienced during those early days of September. In the space of just a few days, life in the shack seemed to move between extremes of insufferable heat to bone-chilling dampness.

We didn't have a lot of time to debate the comfort or discomfort of camp life as we went into last-minute preparations for the much-anticipated annual fall exercise. Everything we had done thus far during the year — from weapons qualifications, to battle fitness tests, to exercises in Haltern and Sennelager — were all done in preparation for the NATO Fall Exercise (Fallex).

The exercise we were about to undertake was completely different than anything we had done before. Fallex would begin in a training area, but after a brief "shake-out" period the balance of the exercise would take place throughout the countryside and small towns of Northern Germany. For the next three weeks we would be living out of our armoured personnel carriers (APCs) and conducting one massive war game over an area roughly 385 miles square.

The logistics for such a massive undertaking are mind boggling. Perhaps a million gallons of fuel would be necessary just to keep the many thousands of wheeled and tracked vehicles of the British Army on the Rhine mobile for the next three weeks. Hundreds of thousands of boxed food rations would be needed to feed the troops. Tons of blank ammunitions would be used to simulate the running battle that was about to take place. The mock war would require units to move great distances each night, and to do this rapidly and accurately each and every vehicle would require up to one hundred maps.

It was no accident that these NATO exercises were always done in the fall. It had nothing to do with military strategy or tactics; it was simply cheaper and less of a burden on the local economy. By early September, the majority of farm crops were already harvested from the ground. Even though the fields were generally free of crops, the damage done still ran into the millions of dollars each year. One squadron of twenty heavy tanks exiting a farmer's field could easily pick up all of the good useable top soil in its tracks and spread it for miles down the road.

I remember one particular occasion where we came across an enemy force dug in at the edge of a small town. When we got into a position to attack, we were faced with what appeared to be a huge field of potatoes. Without so much as a moment's hesitation, our mobile force took off straight across the field. Our combat team consisted of approximately twenty APCs and fifteen Centurion tanks spread out in an extended line that covered an area about 875 yards wide. With every tracked vehicle barrelling forward at full speed through the field, it took us less than three minutes to reach the enemy position. In that same three minutes we completely destroyed the potato crop and probably cost the Canadian government many thousands of dollars in compensation to the farmer.

Later, when we consolidated our position on the outskirts of the little town, I saw the owner of the field. He had a broad smile on his face as he and one of our damage control people were surveying the mess we had made. I thought the smile was a bit odd under the circumstances, but I found out later that he had every reason to smile. Not only would he be paid the full value for the lost crop, but we had saved him the trouble of harvesting it.

On another occasion our APC ran over a chicken, which initially made the farmer very angry and upset, but his demeanour changed quickly when he was told that not only would we pay for the chicken, but also for what would have been its projected egg outlay for the remainder of its life.

On a cool, blustery morning in mid September, our long procession of APCs headed down the road to the railhead in Soest. The day before had been spent loading our four platoon-tracked vehicles with all the equipment and personal kit we would require for the next three weeks. By then I had done a fair amount of travelling in APCs, but this would be the first time I actually got to stand in the hatch and command the vehicle. Doubt about my decision to volunteer began to creep into my brain when Donny Gallant reminded me that there was a good deal more to this job than just standing upright in a hatch. In fact, the real work would only begin after we got to the rail yard.

The first light of dawn was breaking in the east as we roared through the northern fringes of the city. I stood there huddled down in the hatch, trying to shield my face from the biting early-morning wind. The quiet patience of the German people never failed to amaze me. Here we were, driving through their city at the first light of day, with the hammering noise of metal tracks on cobblestone streets and the deafening roar of over a hundred diesel engines resounding off the buildings, and no one complained.

On many occasions during the exercise we would stop for the night in the lanes and alleys of German villages or in the middle of some farmer's barnyard, and only very rarely would we hear even the smallest complaint. Many mornings we woke up to find a pot of coffee or a tray of eggs sitting on the vehicle ramp. The guys always kept some chocolate from the rations to give to the many kids who crowded around the APC every time we stopped. I shudder to think of how Canadians would deal with things if the situation were reversed. I believe that if the average Canadian woke up one morning to find a thirty-ton tank sitting on their driveway and soldiers pitching a tent in their front yard, the initial reaction would be anything but welcoming.

By the time we finally reached the railhead, it was well past first light. Thankfully the sun was out as we alighted from the APCs and busied ourselves sorting out all the chains and metal wedges we would need to securely fasten the vehicles to the train cars. After what seemed an endless series of backwards and forwards manoeuvres, the locomotive finally got the long line of flatbed cars into position against the cement ramp.

One by one, each APC driver was given the hand signal to move forward by his ground guide. Thankfully we were about the twentieth in line, so I had

Moving heavy vehicles and equipment through the narrow confines of a German village could be tricky and often required the assistance of the military police for traffic control.

the benefit of watching and learning what to do. When our turn came, Donny gave me a wink of assurance as I carefully walked up the steep ramp with the APC slowly following.

Donny had joked earlier that the first step onto the train was always a bit unnerving, and he was right. As our vehicle reached the top of the ramp I was already halfway down the car. The weight and momentum of the APC finally caused it to tilt downward, striking the wooded floor of the railcar. I could actually feel the entire floor sag under the sudden weight of the vehicle. The groaning and creaking of the wood under the metal tracks was a little disconcerting as our ten-ton machine slowly inched ahead. The front and rear tailgate of each car had been lowered to create one continuous pathway down the length of the train. As we cautiously moved on to each tailgate, the vehicle's weight would once again drop down onto the next car and the groaning and creaking would begin anew.

It took us the better part of forty minutes to negotiate the entire length of the rail cars and finally reach our tie down position. As Donny inched the vehicle ahead, my job was to jam the metal wedges into position under the front and rear of the vehicle tracks, thereby preventing any movement while the train was in motion. Once they were firmly wedged into place, all that remained was to tighten the vehicle chains down securely to the floor of the railcar. We were both tired and grateful when the German train master finally came by, inspected our work, and pronounced it "Gut!"

I thought we had a difficult job, but as we were finishing our work, I watched as some armoured soldiers were doing basically the same thing as us, only with a squadron of tanks.

Although the APC was only a fraction narrower than the rail car, at least we had a short wall down either side of the car to prevent our APCs from tipping over the edge. The Centurion tank is much wider than an APC, so the short side wall had to be removed to accommodate the extra width.

I was actually nervous just watching as each Centurion tank slowly crawled forward on the railcar with about a foot of track hanging over both edges. Even the slightest miscalculation on the part of the driver or ground guide could result in the tank toppling off the side.

When dawn broke on the following day, it was quite a sight to see. After offloading our train, we moved just a couple of miles to a large, open field to await the arrival of the remaining vehicles. Once all the battalion's wheeled and tracked vehicles were in position, the command to move out sent our huge convoy roaring to life. The sound of over a hundred running engines was deafening, as each of the companies jockeyed to get all of their vehicles in line and ready to go.

The Soltau training area was a relatively isolated stretch of land, not far south of the city of Hamburg. Like almost every military reserve, the land was generally rocky and barren, making it quite useless for any type of agricultural growth. If rocks and boulders were an edible product, a farmer could definitely find a bountiful harvest in this desolate place. Luckily we didn't have much time to contemplate our surroundings. Each of the platoons in support company had been left alone to practice their own specialty before the major exercise began.

Because our platoon had already used most of our annual entitlement of explosives in Sennelager, we now spent all of our time doing some much less exciting dry training in mine warfare.

Mine warfare encompasses two extremely diverse skills. One requires a fair amount of mathematical intelligence, while the other only requires a good deal of brawn and the load-carrying ability of a mule.

Before a single mine goes in the ground, you must first lay out a series of lines and angles using a compass. You start from a fixed point on the map and, after pacing out the required distance, you must determine the angle, bearing, and distance for each and every strip and row of mines you intend to lay. All of this must be done with painstaking precision to ensure that months or even years after the minefield is done, you could still return and know, down to the inch, the exact location of every single live mine.

Once all the math work was done, you could rest your tired brain and pick up a shovel. After lugging the first two fifty-pound anti-tank mines to the start point, you simply dug a deep, saucer-shaped hole for each. Once it was in the hole and armed, you fill the dirt back in and do your best to camouflage the location. All you have to do then is repeat the process for perhaps hundreds of times, depending on the length and depth of the minefield.

When all the bull labour is done, it's time to put your brain back to work, as you take all of your calculations and transfer them onto a minefield recording form. This drawing must be extremely accurate and completed to an exact scale, so that when the hostilities finally end the form can be used to safely locate and recover the mines. Once the form is done, it is held at army headquarters and classified NATO SECRET.

Our last day in the Saltau training area was spend on the mundane tasks associated with cleaning up and getting ready for the final phase of the Fallex.

Our section had been assigned to work with Bravo Company, whom we were scheduled to join up with sometime before last light that evening.

Just before dawn broke the following morning, the Bravo Company combat team crossed the start line and began the long advance through the German countryside, searching for our elusive enemy.

Once the exercise had started, we became completely tactical, meaning that once darkness fell, there was to be no artificial light of any kind used. Had we been in the open, this would not have been a big problem, but we were positioned deep in the woods under a camouflage net. One night, our section commander had been called to the commander's APC to get orders. Although we couldn't see him, we could track his progress back by his long string of curses as he stumbled forward through the intense darkness. When we finally caught sight of his silhouetted figure, he was slowly prodding ahead with both arms extended as he carefully searched the air in front of him, looking a little like a miniature version of the Frankenstein monster. Only after he climbed inside the APC and closed the hatches could we at last turn on the red interior lights.

By the end of day three of the exercise, our bodies were running on fumes. We hadn't actually done that much physical work, but we had travelled over 125 miles with only some very brief stops. For those of us in back of the APC, it wasn't so bad. At least we could curl up on the seat and get some sleep. Our driver, Donny Gallant, looked like death warmed over. Every time we stopped, you could see his head almost instantly tilt forward into sleep. When the word to move came over the radio, our section commander would have to reach forward and shake Donny hard to get up and moving. As the days wore on, it became harder and harder to get him to wake up.

Most meals consisted of opening a can of cold stew or beans and wolfing it down as we continued the advance forward. Whenever we did stop, the tactical procedure was clearly laid down. Vehicles would remain spread out, and pull off the road and into cover under the trees. No one knew how long we would remain stationary. Sometimes it was less than three minutes, and other times we could sit there for over an hour.

Each stop was met with a few moments of indecision. If five minutes passed without a signal to move, we would automatically grab the stove, fire it up, and try to boil a billycan of water for coffee on one burner, while putting an open can of food on the other. Despite our best efforts, most of the coffee and meals we tried to make those first few days ended up being hastily discarded over the side of the vehicle as the order to move came over the radio.

At last we received orders to halt, while another unit passed through our position and took the lead. The entire company moved into this small village and settled in for what we were told would be a minimum of a ten-hour wait. By then our little group was like a well-oiled machine. In less than thirty minutes, our vehicle was backed up against a barn, with the camouflage net draped over the exposed side and a large pot of stew bubbling on the stove.

The British rations we had were not the best, but at least they were filling. Their proper name was "Composition Rations," but we simply referred to them as "Compos." The problem was that where most rations were packaged to feed one man for one day, these rations were put together in bulk and meant to feed an entire section of men, which made it difficult to break down by individual. The difficulty was that regardless of whether you liked something or not, everyone had to eat the same thing. Many of the choices available were somewhat foreign to us. A can of liver and onions or kidney and peas may have been very appetizing to a Brit, but I had difficulty getting past the smell. Each daily ration also contained a can of Oatmeal Blocks, which had about the same taste and consistency as a hockey puck. They were difficult to chew, but if you smeared it with a thick layer of marmalade, at least they had a little taste.

Some of the ration boxes contained a can of Cadbury chocolate bars, which we saved for bartering. Almost as soon as we stopped, the kids would crowd around our APC, curious to see who we were and what we had to trade. It took only a little sign language and some finger math to strike a bargain.

After some rapid talk between themselves, one of the bigger boys would take off down the road, yelling something back to us just before disappearing around the corner. We couldn't understand the words, but the meaning was clear. "Don't give anything away until I get back!" His return trip was done a little more carefully, as he balanced a cardboard tray of twenty-four eggs. Once he had the five chocolate bars in his hands, he immediately bolted away with all the other kids chasing behind, screaming for their share of the loot.

Carrying raw eggs around inside a moving vehicle is not a particularly smart thing to do, but once they were hardboiled we had something that would last for days and could be easily eaten on the move. Unfortunately, with all of us eating hardboiled eggs the air inside the vehicle could and would get rather rancid, but that was a small price to pay for having fresh food.

• • •

I managed to draw the first shift of sentry duty and headed off to my post, while the others curled up to sleep beside the APC. There was an unwritten rule that the driver and section commander always got the bench seats inside the vehicle and right next to the radio set, which had to remain on at all times. The rest of us were free to sleep in any nearby spot, as long as we were within earshot of the vehicle. After three days on the move, anything flat and dry piece of ground would do just fine.

From my sentry post on the nearby road, I could clearly hear the low, continuous crackle of radio static and the steady chorus of heavy snoring coming from under the camouflage net. My legs felt heavy and sore as I prodded back and forth along the edge of the road. The long stone wall bordered the entrance to the farm yard looked very inviting, but I dared not sit down. There was no rule against sitting down on sentry duty, but in my state of fatigue I knew I had to keep moving in order to stay awake and alert.

Luckily for me, I was up and mobile when the sergeant major came by to check on our security. I felt rather silly pointing my rifle at him and asking for the password, but this was part of the game we had to play. I had heard stories where he had approached a sentry and when he was challenged, he just laughed and told the sentry, "Don't worry about it young fella. It's just me." If the sentry accepted this by lowering his weapon and allowing the sergeant major to pass without the password, he was in for a world of trouble. As soon as he reached the sentry unchallenged, he would rip into him verbally and usually end up placing the poor sod on charge for dereliction of duty.

Just before departing, the sergeant major asked if our section wanted to be included in the company brotchen order. Aside from gasthofs, the one other establishment you could find in every German town and village was at least one bakery. Although they made a huge variety of delicious baked goods, the one thing we all loved above everything else was those small, round, white buns known as brotchens. Our request for two dozen was added to the rest of the company's order, for a total of some sixty dozen brotchen. I am sure the baker in that little village must have thought his ship had come in and he was about to make a fortune as he toiled all night to have all those buns ready for pick up early the next morning.

I don't remember much after my three-hour shift ended. Within minutes I was in the sack and fast asleep. It may have been as late as 4:00 a.m., I'm not sure, but suddenly the radio came to life with some panicking voice ordering a "crash harbour."

This particular radio command was only used if there was some dire situation requiring us to get out of our current location as fast as humanly possible. When this order came, the automatic assumption was that the enemy was about to over-run our position, or that a massive enemy artillery bombardment was eminent.

It took a second to comprehend just what was going on, but our section commander was already standing at the edge of the ramp screaming into the darkness. "Get your asses out of the sack and move! I want to be out of here in two minutes, so let's get it in gear!" By then we were all scrambling around, trying to get dressed. Our section commander had quickly acknowledged the radio transmission, and he jumped around, trying to find his map and flash-light. Freddy looked quite comical standing there shouting orders, with only his boots and boxer shorts on. It is ridiculous to think we could do this in two minutes, but considering the circumstances we were working amazingly fast. Only about three minutes had elapsed since the alarm had sounded, and already we had pulled down the camouflage net and tied it down on top on the vehicle. Sleeping bags and kit were literally thrown up the ramp and jammed into any free space available. Donny was already in the driver's compartment, and after starting the engine, he immediately raised the rear ramp. The APC lurched ahead, with our corporal, still in his boots and underwear, guiding it out to the main road.

Advancing toward an unseen enemy in the woods.

Once we reached the rally point in a wood line about three miles to the rear, we could at last relax and catch our breath. We hadn't been the first ones there, but thankfully we were far from last. Bravo Company was well spread out in the dense cover of the tree line. From our vantage point on the high ground, we could barely see the faint outline of the village we had just left. As daylight broke we could hear the sound of tanks and heavy equipment moving through the village and heading in our direction. Judging by the ever increasing amount of radio traffic, it appeared that the companies on our left and right were engaged in a running battle.

The excitement of the early morning soon turned to boredom, as we continued to sit and listen to the battle raging all around us. Everyone was wide awake and alert during those first few early morning hours, but by then most of the guys were dozing in and out of sleep, just waiting for something, anything, to happen.

We had already polished off about half our supply of hardboiled eggs, but without some hot coffee the cold, dry lumps of yolk were not sitting that well in my stomach. It wasn't until Donny mentioned making a sandwich that I suddenly remembered our brotchen order. At first I was a little pissed off that we had missed the chance of getting those nice, fresh buns, but then I felt really bad for that poor baker who was obviously stuck with sixty dozen brotchen and not a paying customer in sight.

We had debated all morning whether or not to brew up some coffee, but as luck would have it, no sooner had the water began to bubble when the company commander's voice booming over the radio. "Prepare to move!"

The reason for the sudden order became instantly apparent as Freddy pointed down the valley. A troop of four American M60 tanks appeared line-a-breast, just forward of the village. Almost at the same time, four more tanks crested the rise just south of us. Judging by the noise and dust clouds, it looked like at least a full squadron of tanks was about to break the cover of the village and come straight for us. Even though they were U.S. forces, we knew they were the enemy by the red flag flying from the antenna and the large red crosses taped on both sides of each vehicle.

Thirty lightly armoured personnel carriers were absolutely no match for a squadron of M60 tanks. The radio instantly crackled to life with the order to withdraw. We could see the company commander's vehicle as he slowly worked his way forward to assess the oncoming threat. The remainder of the vehicles slowly backed off the ridge, taking care not to expose themselves unnecessarily.

Once we were back in the low ground, each vehicle quickly fell into line and headed back to the main road for the rapid withdrawal north.

Up to this point in the mock war we had felt rather useless, as we just continually followed along near the back of the combat team. On the second day there had been one brief moment of excitement when we were ordered forward to check a suspected minefield that was blocking the company's route of advance. When we arrived to survey the situation, the exercise controller was already there. After a quick look around, all we found were a few scattered anti-tank mines along the shoulder of the road. The exercise controller's decision was that all the vehicles were safe as long as they remained in the centre of the road. The prospect of having something exciting to do turned into the rather mundane task of simply erecting a couple of signs to warn vehicles to stay in the middle of the roadway.

Naturally, this being peacetime, no live explosives or munitions of any kind could be used. The job of the exercise controller, or umpire, was to assess the actions of both sides and try and instill some sense of realism into the mock battle. His best tool for accomplishing this was usually by imposing some sort of time restriction. So, for example, during the advance, if we came across a bridge marked as being destroyed, the umpire's job was to assess just how long, in real time, it would take to repair, and that's the amount of time we would have to wait before crossing.

The noise of the enemy tank squadron was quickly drowned out as we made our way back to the north. Just when we had resigned ourselves to yet another long day of driving, the radio voice of the company commander ordered our lone vehicle to pull over to the side of the road and await further instructions.

The sounds of the Bravo Company vehicles were slowly fading in the distance. For a few minutes, the only sound came from our APC idling at the side of the road. Even the distinctive sound made by the enemy tanks could no longer be heard. We just sat there on the side of the road, feeling rather exposed and vulnerable. Even our normally self-assured section commander looked slightly perplexed and a little nervous about sitting there alone in the open.

Just as we thought that perhaps we had been forgotten, the radio once again came to life. Our orders were simple. The enemy was being held up by an artillery barrage that had destroyed three or four of their lead tanks, and we were to delay their advance even further by blowing a crater in the main road.

Had we been doing this for real, the task of blowing a hole deep and wide enough to prevent the passage of a tank would take approximately one hour.

Our mock simulation of laying out tape and signing the area as "destroyed" took just fifteen minutes to complete. Our exercise umpire arrived as we were finishing our task and told us we must sit for one hour, after which we could call in and report the road destroyed and the task complete.

When we left our crater task, all the section commander was given was a six-figure map reference to try and find Bravo Company, who were at the time held up in a heavily wooden area, some 25 miles north of us. I have to say we were all quite impressed when, after driving all afternoon and going through three separate map sheets, he guided us to the exact location.

Thankfully we were able to settle into our new location, deep in the forest, before nightfall. By early evening it was pitch black, and we felt around, trying to fix the camouflage net and organize our kit, all without showing any artificial light. There may have been a moon that night, but the thick canopy of branches above prevented any light from reaching us. Unlike the first night in the woods, we were a little better prepared and could manage to get most things sorted out, despite the total blackness.

There is an old saying in the army: "Never sit up when you can lie down, and never stay awake when you can sleep." With the exception of the sentry, we were all in sleeping bags and fast asleep within fifteen minutes.

"Okay, okay, I'm awake," I mumbled angrily at whomever it was shaking me. I had drawn the 3:00 to 6:00 a.m. sentry shift, but it felt like I'd just shut my eyes.

"Get the hell out of that bag right now!" It still took a few seconds to realize what was going on. It wasn't just me being roused out for my shift on sentry duty. I could see the dark outline of the many APCs parked around us, but with the exception of our little group cursing and swearing in the darkness, nobody else appeared to be moving.

At least we had all been smart enough to only remove our boots before getting in the sleeping bag. All of us sat shivering and confused in the back of the APC, waiting to hear what was going on. Freddy soon returned from receiving orders and told us we were heading over to Delta Company to help erect a protective minefield.

This isn't so bad, I thought. We had all of the soldiers from one of the platoons to carry and bury the mines, while all I had to do was oversee the work party. The original plan had called for a much bigger minefield, but when we arrived we discovered that a large herd of cows were grazing right in the middle of the intended location. After a quick reconnaissance, the decision was made to place the mines in a nearby open pasture where there would be no chance of disturbing the cattle.

Our section commander had the unpleasant job of trying to deal with a young and very arrogant platoon commander, who, in spite of a complete lack of mine laying experience, was still insisting on being in charge. In the distance, I could hear Freddy trying unsuccessfully to convince the young officer that the intricate job of plotting all the necessary bearings and measuring the distances should be left to him. It was hard not to laugh as we listened to the pair of them bickering over who was best qualified to do the job. The battle of wills between these two giant egos was fascinating to watch.

Whether we liked it or not, our section commander was much better qualified to do this job. The young lieutenant staunchly held his ground and refused to allow a mere corporal to dictate to him. Eventually rank won out as Freddy handed over the minefield record form and stomped back to the vehicle.

With such a large work party, the task was completed quickly and we arrived back in our old location just after five o'clock in the morning. Our good corporal was still fuming over the lost confrontation and had not said a word to us on the trip back to Bravo Company. Because we arrived back just at the time I would have been on sentry, I got to start my duty while the rest of the guys stumbled around in the dark, trying to sort everything out and get a little sleep before first light.

Slowly the darkness gave way to the grey mist of dawn. I was completely dog tired but continued to rove back and forth in an effort to stay awake and warm. Thankfully the rain had held off for the past few days, but the early morning mist and dampness seemed to reach through my heavy combat jacket and chill me to the bone. The low buzzing static from the radio and the uninterrupted snoring coming from the APC were the only noises disturbing an otherwise peaceful morning. I envied the guys buried deep in their sleeping bags. I only had an hour left on my shift, but when I finished, daylight would come and the work day would begin anew.

I was so busy looking at my watch for the third time in less than five minutes, that I was momentarily startled by the sound of footsteps crashing through the bush and heading directly for me. "Where the hell is Corporal Howard?" The sergeant major looked quite upset as he stormed passed me without stopping. By the time I told him he was sleeping inside the vehicle, the sergeant major was already on the ramp and yelling for Freddy to wake up. When he finally figured who was standing over him yelling, he leapt out of the sleeping bag and cracked his head on the low metal rack just above his head. Freddy's little mishap seemed to calm the sergeant major down, if only for a second. Freddy has barely said he was okay before the sergeant major lit into him again. "Just what the hell were you thinking?" The sergeant major's tirade continued as our section commander just sat there in open-mouthed disbelief. Freddy's normal self-assurance was completely rattled by the pointed accusation about a problem with the minefield recorder form.

It was Freddy's turn to get upset. "I told that stupid little prick, but he just wouldn't listen!"

"All right, I believe you," the sergeant major finally said, trying to calm things down. "Anyway, the Colonel wants an answer and you're just the guy to explain it to him."

Apparently the young Delta Company officer had filled in all of the proper information on the minefield recorder. He had gone over the form in great detail and made sure that all the compass bearings, lines, and symbols on the drawing were meticulously accurate before sending it off to the brigade head-quarters. Unfortunately, in his zeal to be completely accurate, he sketched in a few additional items not normally found on a minefield recorder form.

Our commanding officer was not a particularly happy man when he was awakened an hour later by the brigade commander and asked to explain why there were little pictures of grazing cows all around the fringes of the drawing.

The old saying that "shit rolls down hill" was very true in this case, as the CO demanded answers from the company commander, who in turn sent his sergeant major to attack our hapless section commander.

When Freddy returned to our vehicle later that morning, he looked calm and relieved, but all he would say was that the situation had been straightened out. When someone brought the subject up later, he was summarily cut off mid-sentence. "The CO knows what really happened and now the subject is closed!" I don't remember it ever being brought up again. It may have been a coincidence, but shortly after we arrived back from the exercise I did see the offending lieutenant's name appear on orders as the base duty officer for fourteen days straight.

• • •

The last few days of the exercise were a blur of non-stop activity. After our hasty withdrawal to the north, we had gone into a defensive mode in the hilly country, some thirty-eight miles west of Hamburg.

Ask any soldier to tell you his least favourite phase of war, and without a doubt he will immediately answer defensive operations. Time can pass very slowly if all you're doing is sitting in a trench and waiting for the enemy to appear. There is nothing exciting about sitting in a hole in the ground, especially if it is cold and raining. During daylight, you must remain relatively stationary behind the camouflage dirt mound at the front of your trench, so as not to give your position away. No fires can be built for warmth or cooking, lest the smoke draw artillery fire down on you. The quartermaster will bring hot food, but only under cover of darkness. One man must remain on lookout in the trench, while the other feels his way back in the dark to pick up some food. With a tiny red-filtered flashlight in one hand and a ladle in the other, the store man carefully shovels food into your mess tins and coffee into your canteen cup. It is impossible to tell what food you are getting. All you can hope for is that it is still semi-warm by the time you juggle and stumble your way back to the trench.

When the enemy finally did appear just after dawn on the fourth day, we were actually grateful for the opportunity to get some action and excitement. The mock battle raged all morning, and then suddenly around midday everything became deathly quiet again. At first it looked like the final attack was about to commence, when suddenly all of the enemy troops pulled back behind their vehicles and mounted up, while the .50-calibre machineguns continued to provide covering fire. The American M60 tanks on the flanks ejected their smoke grenades, blanketing the entire area in a dense grey fog. We could no longer see them, but it was clear by the slowly diminishing sound of engines that the enemy was withdrawing.

By late afternoon, we were once again back on the road and pushing the enemy south. The NATO offensive continued unabated for four more days. The Bravo Company combat team would drive flat out for perhaps a mile or two, then, without warning, we would come to a sudden stop as the reconnaissance platoon reported enemy contact ahead. Once the enemy had been dealt with by the infantry platoons, we would be called forward to clear any mines or obstacles blocking the route. When the exercise umpire declared the area clear, we would once again mount our vehicle and try to catch even a few minutes sleep as the advance continued.

Just after dawn one morning, the commanding officer's voice on the radio net signaled the end of the exercise. "All stations, this is call sign niner. End Ex."

After loading the train in a small village just outside Hanover, we all settled in for the long ride home. The trip took the better part of an entire day, but that didn't matter; most of us were fast asleep before the train even left the station. The first thing we took off was our boots, but even the stench of 150 pairs of smelly feet and unwashed bodies could not keep us awake for even a moment. Just before my head settled against the soft armrest and I fell asleep, the thought struck me that we would all be getting a long weekend off. Some of the guys and I had already decided that with three full days off, there was only one place to go, and that was Amsterdam.

Photo courtesy of the Department of National Defence.

Once the enemy was located, the assault group would move off to the enemy's flank to get ready for the final attack.

Chapter 9

My Home in Amsterdam

It was almost too frightening to watch, but I could not take my eyes off the taxi speedometer as we flew down the highway toward Soest. Our driver was taking full advantage of the fact that there were no speed limits on this or any German highway, as his speedometer needle edged just over the ninety miles an hour mark. Telephone poles and trees went by in a blur. One second I could see the faint pinpricks of headlights from a car approaching from the distance, and the next moment it was by us in a flash of light. My buddies and I may have been just a little terrified, but our taxi driver seemed to be relishing our fear. Of course, the fact that this situation was completely our own fault gave me little comfort as we careened down the highway, cheating death on every curve.

All of this could have been avoided if we had done a decent job of cleaning up in the first place. Instead of giving the tools and equipment a proper cleaning, we had wasted almost the entire afternoon messing around. After failing the first inspection, we had been kept at work for an extra two hours to correct the problems.

The train to Amsterdam was due to depart at six o'clock sharp, and we had left ourselves precious little time to get to the train station in Soest and purchase the tickets. Our death-defying cab ride finally came to a successful end, as our driver squealed to a stop at the front entrance of the train station with less than ten minutes to spare.

It had been a particularly harrowing afternoon, but we had made it. The train was crowded, but after walking the length of four train cars we managed to find an empty compartment. It was with a great sense of relief that I finally could throw my small bag in the rack and flopped into a seat. After the frightening ride and the anxious moments waiting at the ticket counter, I could finally relax and catch my breath. It was obvious by the loud noise emanating from some of the nearby compartments that at least a few guys had gotten here early enough to have a few drinks before the train departed. Judging by the ever increasing noise coming from the passageway, more and more alcohol was being consumed and people were getting a head start on a drunken weekend.

There was a marked decrease in the level of noise as the train got closer to the border. We were all well aware that once the border patrol showed up, we would all have to be on our best behaviour if we expected to cross into Holland. These Dutchmen were quite particular about who entered their country. When they appeared at your compartment, they expected to see your ticket and identification card. If you were too drunk or were stupid enough to give them a hard time, you would quickly find yourself off the train and stuck in the tiny border town until you were sober enough to continue your journey. We knew that we would have no problem in that regard. We hadn't had the time for even one quick beer before departing. We all had a bottle of duty-free liquor tucked away in our bags, but the plan was to only open them once we were safely past the border.

When the train finally chugged to a halt at the border station in Emmerich, Holland, you could hear a pin drop. Five uniformed guards entered each end of the train and began checking paperwork in each compartment, working their way quickly toward the middle. A large, stoic-looking man glanced at each of our ID cards in turn, and after he was satisfied that we actually looked somewhat like our picture, he handed them back and disappeared. We thought the last small hurdle had been passed, and we all sat smiling and waiting for the train to start moving, so that we could have a celebratory drink and toast to a weekend of fun.

We could hear the voice of the border guard demanding identification from someone a couple of compartments down. At first the voice sounded normal, but as he continued to repeatedly demand to see someone's identification, you could hear the frustration as his voice got steadily louder. By then, three or four of the guards had converged in the hallway and all were shouting at the yet unidentified individual. The hallway quickly filled with curious onlookers, all anxious to see the source of the commotion. Someone passed the word down that there was some Canadian passed out in the compartment, and try as they may, the guards could not wake him up.

It was difficult to see what was going on because of the number of people blocking the hallway, but judging by the scuffling noise inside the compartment, it looked like our countryman was about to be taken off the train.

Once the guards physically dragged him out of the compartment, I could see he was completely passed out and obviously unaware of what was happening to him. It took a moment to register, but I soon realized I knew him well. Rick Dingle was a big, strapping guy, who was known throughout the battalion for his hockey prowess. He and I had shared a couple of drinks together on occasion. He was a loud, boisterous person, with a ready wit and booming voice that seemed to fill a room. He was one of those rare individuals who always appeared to be upbeat and able to tackle all that life could throw at him. I think we could have become good friends, but once he became a member of the battalion hockey team, we each moved in different circles.

Once my friends and I realized it was Rick, we immediately tried to help. We forced our way through the crowded hallway, in the hope of getting to the guards and convincing them that we could take care of our unconscious friend.

When we finally reached him, he was already laying face-down on the hallway carpet, just a few feet away from the door. The guards looked extremely agitated, but I did manage to calm them down somewhat, as I tried to explain that I would try to find his ID card. After hurriedly feeling inside all his pockets, I still could not locate his wallet. I next turned to try and find his bag, but it was too late. While I was busy scanning the area, the guard closest to Rick finally ran out of patience and tried waking him with a hard kick to the stomach. Any chance that the situation would be peacefully resolved was now gone, and all hell broke loose.

The guard was about to land a second kick when my friend Pat Gallin floored him with a right hook to the jaw. Zeke Bedard pounced on the back of another guard and slammed him up against the wall. I was still down on all fours when I felt a blow to the back of my head. My arms instinctively came up to protect my head, and the blows continued to rain down on me. After managing to stagger to my feet, I lunged forward, hitting my attacker around the waist and slamming him to the floor. Out of the corner of my eye I caught a glimpse of two more guards dragging the still unconscious Rick to his feet, and throw his limp body off the train from the top step. Despite the bedlam and noise, I could hear the sickening sound of Rick's body hitting the cement platform face first. By then there were six guards all trying desperately to get at the three of us still trapped in the confines of the hallway. One by one we were dragged kicking and fighting from the train. I was just barely hanging onto the door, when a foot caught me square in the chest and propelled me backwards onto the platform. Before I could even catch my breath, one of the guards jumped on top of me and pinned my arms down with his knees. I thought I was about to pass out from the blows raining down across my unprotected face, but Paddy came to my rescue by tackling the guy and forcing him off me.

Up until then the fight had been somewhat even. We may have been out-numbered, but at least we were holding our own. When the train coming from Holland into Germany arrived on the other side of the platform, I knew immediately we were in serious trouble.

Almost as soon as the other train stopped the German border guards came pouring off, with night sticks waving, as they plunged into the maelstrom. In less than a minute it was all over, and the four of us lay bruised and bleeding on the cold platform.

I guess I just assumed that our arrest was imminent, but to our surprise the Dutch and German border guards seemed more interested in getting back on their respective trains and away from us crazy Canadians. As the train pulled away, our getaway bags were unceremoniously thrown off the train. As if I didn't feel bad enough, the sound of my forty-ounce bottle breaking inside my bag as it slammed into the cement just made me sick to my stomach.

We may have been stiff and sore, but that didn't prevent us from making a hasty exit from the train station. I still don't know why the cops didn't show up to arrest the lot of us, but rather than press our luck, we decided to head into town and try and find someplace to clean up and crash out for the night. Zeke was the smallest of us, so he took all the bags while Paddy and I each took one of Rick's arms over our shoulders and started the long walk to the middle of the small town.

Rick had remained completely unconscious throughout the entire incident, but finally, as we approached a promising-looking gasthof, he started to show some signs of movement. Slowly he came to life, and he turned his head and stared at Paddy and me through half-open eyes. We must have looked a sight, with our blood-stained faces, ripped clothes, and sweaty, matted hair. "Where did all the blood come from?" At first I was angry and ready to lash out at the obviously stupid question, but when I turned to respond, all I could see was his look of dazed confusion. The fact that he was utterly oblivious to all that had happened just struck me as completely ludicrous. Paddy and I must have thought the same thing at the same time, because we both began to laugh uncontrollably.

I caught a glimpse of myself in a store window and it was not a pretty sight. Any hotel owner in his right mind would hardly allow us through the door, so if we were going to get off the street for the night we had to come up with a plan. Zeke looked the most presentable, so we sent him in while Paddy, Rick, and I rested on the street curb outside. Fortunately the stairs to our second-floor room were just inside the main entrance, so we were able to get to our room without being seen.

The next morning at first light I awoke suddenly, not remembering where I was. After a few seconds of lying there, it all came back to me. I could hear the groans as each person woke up and tried to get their sore, stiff bodies upright and moving. We had all managed to clean ourselves up somewhat, but judging by the large spot of dried blood on my pillow, it was obvious that my nose must have started bleeding again sometime during the night.

We had no idea of what to expect when we re-entered the train station, but being that we were already just inside the Dutch border, we had little choice but to return to the scene of the crime. Our plan was simply to try and mix with the crowd on the platform and remain as inconspicuous as possible until we could board the train. Everything was going fine until Rick discovered he could not find his ID card. We could still get to Amsterdam, but coming back into Germany would be impossible without this key piece of identification.

Our plan to stay out of sight and as unobtrusive as possible was completely shot, as Rick had no choice but to walk straight into the border control station. Paddy, Zeke, and I sat nervously waiting for him to reappear. At first we had considered getting on the train and leaving, but our guilt about abandoning him kept us sitting there waiting.

After nervously waiting for more than twenty minutes, I took a deep breath of relief as I saw Rick coming out the door with a big broad smile on his face. "Not to worry guys. They have my ID card, but we all need to report to the office before they'll give it to me."

As we all stood by the office counter, I could see three of the guards from the night before. One of them had a clearly visible bruise where Paddy had clocked him in the jaw. After copying our names down from our ID cards, we hurried back to the platform just in time to jump aboard the train.

Although I was quite exhausted, even the rhythmic movement of the train couldn't get me to fall asleep. When I voiced my concern, no one wanted to talk about it. Our little encounter in the border control office earlier that morning had gone far too easily. I could not shake the feeling of dread. I wanted to believe that the whole incident was behind us, but common sense and logic told me that our problems were far from over.

• • •

Amsterdam's main train station is a huge Gothic structure, with massive pillars supporting a classically designed dome roof. If not for the sound of train whistles and the noise of bustling foot traffic hurrying about the station, one could easily mistake it for a cathedral.

As soon as we reached the main concourse, we began scanning the area for the man we were looking for. It didn't take long to spot the lineup of men in the centre of the main hall, each holding hand written signs. According to the signs, there was no shortage of hotels from which we could choose. Some of the guys swore by the Continental Hotel, others would only stay at the State Side, but for most Canadians their first choice would always be the My Home Hotel.

My Home may have been called a hotel, but it was really much more like a large, family-run boarding house. After the eldest son drove us from the train station, we were met by his mother in the hotel's front hallway. I have no idea what her name was, because all of us who knew her just simply called her "Mama." She was a wonderful, caring woman, and must have been in her late fifties at the time.

Mama's smiling face changed to a look of deep concern when she came down the narrow hallway to greet us at the front desk. Paddy and I had taken the brunt of the punishment in the fight, and each of us sported some dark bruises around the nose and eyes. The side of Rick's face looked like raw meat, with long, red scratches and a swollen cheek from where his face had impacted with the platform. After telling the somewhat sterilized version of the story, she just looked at us for a long while. I am sure she knew there was probably more to it than we were saying, but she didn't press the issue. After a brief lecture on staying out of trouble, she insisted we go into the kitchen and eat some leftover breakfast.

Downtown Amsterdam was completely different from any city I had seen before. Everywhere you looked there was water. Numerous boats and barges puttered along the canal that paralleled the main street. When we reached the first cross street, we waited patiently for the light to change, while thousands of bicycles filled the intersection. What few cars there were all seemed to be North American, straight out of the 1950s. As the light changed, the teeming sea of bicycle and foot traffic all seemed to move like a well-synchronized ballet.

The whole ebb and flow of traffic was fascinating to watch. Without all the cars and trucks, most of the normal street sounds were absent. The noise and smell of engines and the sound of car horns had been replaced by the more tranquil ringing of bicycle bells. I was almost sorry when we turned off the main street and headed down a narrow lane in search of our first of many beer stops that evening.

After a couple of beers in the 51st State Bar, we stopped for some food at one of the many little cafés along Canal Street. For some strange reason, the majority of these places seemed to have an extremely limited menu, consisting of only hamburgers, bratwurst, french fries, and pea soup. The man behind the counter looked a bit annoyed when I returned my hamburger and asked him to cook it. It wasn't that it was undercooked, it just wasn't cooked at all. After putting it on the grill for all of a minute, he returned the semi-pink patty to me with a big smile. Of course, I didn't know that a hamburger in Holland consisted of raw meat and raw onions served on a bun. I waited for him to turn around before depositing the raw meat in the garbage and eating just the empty bun.

After dark, the streets were a buzz of excitement and activity. We stopped on the corner to watch and listen to an organ grinder play, while his monkey moved through the crowd collecting cash donations. Further down the road, another small group of curious onlookers were taking beer bets on and against Fred Boucher. One American sailor was loudly proclaiming he would buy everyone a beer if Fred succeeded in his attempt to walk down the center of the laneway — on his hands! Fred hesitated for just a moment and then ran back into the bar. Just as the Yank started smiling, thinking he had won, Fred re-emerged with two stubby beer bottles. He leaned forward, carefully placing his hands around the bottles, and after a moment's concentration, he effortlessly raised himself into a full handstand, using both bottles as a firm base. After a few seconds to steady his balance, he proceeded to walk down the lane on the beer bottles. Even the Yank had to admit it was quite a show, and he bought a round of beer for the house.

It was getting close to midnight when Zeke and I finally headed out the door. The Derby was definitely the best bar we had been in all night, and I almost hated to leave. Our original plan had been to stay right there until closing time, but we overheard a couple of drunks talking at the bar about a contest scheduled for later that night in the barroom of the Continental Hotel. I had heard about these daredevil contests before, but had a hard time believing they actually happened. After all, who could possibly be stupid enough to do such a thing?

We emerged back onto Canal Street on our way to the Continental. Not surprisingly, the street was packed with foot traffic, all doing what the locals referred to as "window shopping." The predominately male crowd continued to meander back and forth, stopping every so often to try and strike up a bargain with one of the many ladies sitting in the showroom windows. Prostitution was not only legal in Holland, but also under government control. This street was at the very heart of Amsterdam's red light district, and being Saturday night, it looked like half the male population of the city was prowling the area. For someone brought up in holy catholic Ireland and raised in "Toronto the Good," this was an incredible sight to behold. It felt a little like walking past the huge display windows of a department store, except instead of seeing brightly displayed jewellery or fashionably dressed mannequins, these were real human beings for sale. The largest crowds of men seemed to gather in front of the first few windows, where the girls were the youngest and prettiest. As you moved down the street, the crowd slowly petered out as the women got older and less attractive. Young or old, they all looked rather sad and bored. Listening to them bargaining with a customer, you could almost believe you were in a grocery store, listening to people dickering over the price of a loaf of bread or a pound of meat.

It took a while to fight our way through the throng of busy shoppers, but once we crossed the bridge, the crowd all but disappeared.

The Continental Hotel backed right up against the canal. The rear of the four-storey building actually formed the canal boundary wall. From the windows in the hotel barroom, you could look straight down to the water.

As soon as we walked through the door, we were greeted loudly by a group of howling drunks who insisted we join them. As we moved toward their table in the back corner of the barroom, I recognized Garry Collin and Gil Johnson from Delta Company, but the other two guys were unfamiliar to me. We had obviously walked in at the tail end of a heated discussion, but it only took a few minutes to figure out that the contest was about to begin.

"Twenty guilders says neither of you will do it!" One of them slapped the money on the table, daring Collins or Johnson to pick it up.

"For twenty guilders? Are you kidding? Make it fifty and we'll both do it!" The original better paused and looked around the table at all of us. He may have been drunk, but fifty guilders was still a lot of money. It was like watching a good poker match, with the better staring at his opponents, trying to detect if they were bluffing. Collins and Johnson just sat there, crossed armed and smiling, waiting for him to take the bet or fold. For a moment it looked like he was about to fold and take back his twenty guilders, when the fourth member of the group spoke up.

"I'll throw in ten guilders, if you guys will match it," he said, looking at Zeke and me for support.

Zeke and I just looked at each other and shrugged. "What the hell," I said, reaching for my wallet. I thought I saw a moment of doubt in their eyes, but they quickly stood up, grabbed the fifty guilders off the table, and began to strip.

Time was of the essence. This little stunt would have to be done quickly, before the bartender saw what was happening and tried to stop it. Garry and Gil stayed partially hidden near the back corner as they quickly stripped down to their underwear. After a last glance around the room to confirm nobody was watching, one of the guys pulled back the latch and flung open the big bay window. The sudden gust of wind drew the attention of the bartender, who only had time to look, as both guys quickly climbed out on the ledge and leapt feet first into the canal, some thirty feet below.

By then the bartender was yelling and screaming something about insane Canadians, but we were too busy craning our necks out the window, trying to make sure we saw two heads bob to the surface. It was dark and difficult to see, but finally both heads emerged from the gloomy water and began the slow, cold swim to the far bank.

It was probably just bad luck, but as the first guy got to the ladder and started to climb out on the far bank, a cop on horseback came around the corner.

The cops in this particular part of Amsterdam were anything but friendly. When you consider that the area they patrolled contained nothing but whore-houses, cheap hotels, tattoo parlours, and seedy bars, all catering to soldiers, sailors, and hookers, it was easy to understand why the police might be a little cranky. Rarely a night went by without at least twenty or thirty arrests for drunkenness, fighting, or causing some kind of disturbance. Although the police carried guns, they rarely used them, preferring instead to use a short sharp sword to poke you into submission. If you are being held against a wall by a horse's flank while a sword is being pressed into your chest, it is difficult, if not extremely stupid, to resist.

The small crowd let out a cheer as each guy flashed the peace sign and climbed aboard the paddy wagon for the short drive to jail. Had they known what awaited them they probably would have reconsidered the whole stupid stunt. The waters of Amsterdam's many canals served not only as a mode of transport for boats and barges, but also made up an intricate part of the city's sewer system. Immediately after arriving at the police station, they were ordered to strip naked and stand facing the wall. As soon as they got in position, they were hosed down with a high pressure fire hose. After a minute of this, they were ordered to turn around, so the soaking could be repeated. Johnson told me later that he thought the force of the water was going to peel his skin away.

Once the cops were satisfied that every inch of skin had been cleaned, they were marched naked and wet into another room where a rather large man in a white coat ordered them to bend over. As soon as they complied, they were instantly stabbed in the buttocks with a long hypodermic needle. After receiving this tetanus shot they were allowed to get dressed before being handed a blanket and placed in a cell for the remainder of the night.

After each paying a ten guilder fine, they were released just in time to catch the early morning train back to Germany.

Mama seemed genuinely sorry to see us all leave. By early Sunday morning her little kitchenette was filled to capacity, while practically the entire population of the hotel tried to shovel down some breakfast before departing.

Although I had great time on this my first trip to Amsterdam, those feelings of dread returned as we headed off to catch the noon train back to Germany. Perhaps if I had known what awaited us back in Fort York, I would not have slept quite so soundly on the long train ride home.

Chapter 10
"Merry Christmas – Quick March!"

O ne bitterly cold morning in mid December we all stood shivering and anxious for the inspection to end so that we could get back inside. Sergeant Stoke had been particularly slow that morning, and I could already feel a tingling sensation in my ears as the cold wind swirled around us. At last he moved out front to pronounce the magic words which would send us charging back inside the heated building. "Private Burke, stand fast. Remainder, fall out!" Suddenly I was standing there alone.

"Burke, the sergeant major wants to see you at the company office." My mind immediately began racing through all the variables. Common sense told me that there could be any number of reasons why he would want to see me, but I was suddenly filled with a feeling of impending doom. I could have asked the sergeant, but it felt like I already knew and didn't want to hear my fears confirmed. Sergeant Stoke saw my momentary hesitation, but only told me to get a move on.

As soon as I came to attention in front of the sergeant major's desk, I could see from the expression on his face that my worst fears were about to be confirmed. "This just came in this morning from the military police," he said as he opened a file folder and scanned the forms inside. All I could do was watch as his face muscles slowly contorted while he continued to read. By the time he finished, I could already feel the small beads of sweat forming on my forehead. Any faint hope I had of this being something else was dashed with his next words. "Looks like you and your friends got yourselves in some trouble with the Dutch border police." I could tell by his tone that this was more a statement than a question, but still my mind raced, trying to think of something meaningful to say. Nothing came to me. I just stood there waiting for the axe to fall. After a few moments' reflection, he stood up and threw the file folder back into his basket. "Right, I'll be talking to the other culprits soon and passing this to the company commander this afternoon." I just stood there dumbly, waiting to be dismissed. "You can carry on Burke, but as of this moment consider yourself on charge. You and your friends can expect to go before the company commander for trial within the week."

A summary trial is the military's way of dealing with most types of offences in an expeditious manner. If the charge is serious enough, the person will be asked if we wishes to be court-martialled or if he is willing to accept the finding of the company commander. Most opt for the latter because a court martial can take days, sometimes weeks, to complete, where the majority of summary trials take less than an hour.

The accused individual is marched in front of his company commander, where the charge is read and evidence is given. If the charge is simple and straightforward, the accused will be asked to give his side of the story. Witnesses may be called to give evidence, but once the company commander has heard all sides, he then pronounces sentence. The powers of punishment for a company commander are somewhat limited, but his findings can range from a dismissal of the charges, to a fine of up to two hundred dollars, to confinement to barracks, or as much as fourteen days in jail.

Although the military law systems and procedures have become much more tightly controlled and restrictive over the past couple of decades, in the 1960s the system can best be described as a real crap shoot. Sentences could range from being plain silly to the absolute barbaric, depending on the particular whims of the company commander you appeared before.

Most, if not all of these commanders were highly trained and efficient soldiers. The majority had been in Korea and had spent more than twenty years perfecting their leadership skills. Unfortunately, none of them had any legal training and preferred to determine guilt or innocence using some very unique and strange methods.

The officer commanding Alfa Company had a large bulldog who always sat beside his desk throughout a summary trial. Once all the evidence had been heard and just before he pronounced sentence, the company commander would turn to the dog and ask his opinion on what had just transpired. As all the soldiers knew, if the dog lay there quietly, chances were you would get off lightly. However, if the dog raised its head and let out even the slightest growl, you were obviously guilty and about to be hammered with a stiff sentence.

We had another company commander who truly hated everything about the pay corps and would look for any opportunity to stick it to them. When a soldier was found guilty of an offence and given a fine, the amounts were normally rounded out to an even number. In those days' of little pay, a fine usually ranged from $10 for something minor, to perhaps $200 for something more serious. This particular major always gave fines in odd amounts, like $10.22 or $99.01, so that the pay clerks had slightly more difficulty calculating and balancing their books.

Major Roland in Bravo Company had two small quirks when it came to administering military justice. It was well known that if you appeared before him and could come up with a story he had never heard before, chances of getting off free were generally good. There was a story of one particular individual who had been charged on exercise for killing and eating a chicken. "Well, you see, sir, I was patrolling back and forth in this farm yard on sentry duty one night. All of a sudden I heard this noise behind me, and when I turned around this chicken was stalking me. When I stopped, he stopped. When I started to walk again, he would continue to stalk me from behind. When I finally turned around to confront the chicken, it suddenly lunged straight for my neck. We wrestled for a while, but I finally killed it in self defence." The soldier was told to be more careful around chickens in the future and the case was dismissed.

When Major Roland thought the person before him was in need of a life lesson, he would offer them two choices: accept the fine or confinement he was about to pronounce, or step out behind the building for an old fashioned ass kicking. I don't know of anyone who actually took him up on his offer to step outside. Perhaps it was because the major was known throughout the battalion for having been an exceptionally good heavyweight boxer in his younger days.

Unfortunately for us, the officer commanding support company was an unknown entity. He had only arrived from Canada a few weeks earlier and little was known about him. On the one occasion I had actually spoken to him it was to salute and say good morning as I passed on the road. I all got in return was a half hearted salute and a grunt as he hurried past me.

When the fateful morning finally arrived, we found ourselves standing rigidly at attention in front of the company commander's desk.

Just minutes earlier, standing in the hallway, we had been given our first of many surprises that day. Paddy, Zeke, and I were to be charged under article 119 of Queens Regulations, for "Conduct to the Prejudice of Good Order and Discipline," for creating an international incident. What I found truly shocking was that Rick Dingle was only being charged with "drunkenness" and would be tried separately.

The three of us stood silently before the commander's desk, listening as the formal charge statement was read. Once the sergeant major finished, we were each asked, in turn, if we wished a summary trial or court martial. After we all choose the former, the trial began immediately.

Although there were no witnesses present, the written statements of the border guards were pretty damning. Not surprisingly, they didn't mention anything about flinging Rick's limp body face-first onto the platform. Nor did the statements contain a word about the guard sitting on my chest and pummeling me with his night stick. It did, however, talk about all of us being very drunk and refusing to cooperate when asked for identification.

I have no idea what the others were feeling, but this entire proceeding was definitely not going the way I had imagined. Judging by the look of disgust on the company commander's face as the statements were read, I knew we were almost certainly doomed. When we were finally asked to speak, it felt like it was being done as part of the necessary procedure, rather than an attempt to get at the truth.

Zeke started to say something about how we were only trying to help Private Dingle, but no sooner had he gotten the name out of his mouth and he was cut off abruptly. "We aren't here to discuss Private Dingle's behaviour. He'll be dealt with later. What I want to know is why you three drunken morons shouldn't be locked up!" With that statement from the company commander, I should have known our fate was sealed, but I just couldn't let it go.

"Excuse me, sir, but we weren't drunk," I said weakly. My words only served to make him angrier.

"Well, if that's true, how do you explain why the statement says that you all reeked of booze?" He kept staring at me, while tapping the statement lying on his desk. Until then we had all been standing at attention, staring straight ahead. I opened my mouth to try and explain how the smell of booze was caused by the bottles breaking when the guards threw our bags off the train, but I already knew it was no use. Nobody was listening. Our good major had probably decided our collective guilt before we even entered the room.

After a few more minutes of ranting, the company commander finally pronounced sentence. "I find all of you guilty and sentence you to fourteen days detention. Sergeant major, get these people out of my sight!"

After spending our first night in confinement, we were scheduled to be moved to the detention barracks by noon the following day. Being constantly surrounded by MPs, the three of us had not been able of speak more than a few scattered words to each other. The entire morning had been spent clearing out of the battalion. For all intents and purposes, we were no longer soldiers. We were convicts and would be treated as such, at least for the next two weeks.

During the out clearance one of the more sadistic MPs took great pleasure in passing on some news to us. Rick Dingle, the guy we had been so willing to defend, had gone on trial shortly after us. He had been found guilty of being "drunk in a public place" and was given a $50 fine.

When the time finally came to depart, there was one final minor glitch. Apparently I had been overpaid in September, and I would have to remain in the guardroom for another night while the paperwork was sorted out. Under normal circumstances the problem would have been corrected and the extra fifteen dollars paid back in less than a week, but because a prisoner's pay was only 25 cents a day, the books would take nearly a month to balance.

Paddy and Zeke had been moved the day before, so I would be the only passenger for the ride to the detention centre. Fortunately for me, I was given a bit of a reprieve on the short journey north.

There was a shortage of military policemen in the brigade, so my escort was actually a member of the battalion working as a regimental policeman. Some of these RPs could actually be worse than the military police they worked for, but John Bennett was one of the good ones.

Just after we passed Fort Henry, we turned right onto a gravel road that led to our final destination. John and I knew each other, but so far on the trip he had said nothing. I realized the situation was a little awkward for both of us, so I remained silent as well. Our quiet ride continued until we reached the tree line, about 550 yards from the gate of the detention centre. Suddenly, without warning, John pulled the vehicle to the side of the gravel road and stopped. "Here," he said, reaching into his pocket. "Have one of these. It's probably the last one you get for the next couple of weeks." I was a bit dumbfounded, but nonetheless grateful for his small generosity.

"Thanks," was all I could say as he handed me a cigarette.

I knew that if we were seen, John could get in trouble for his kindness, so I tried to smoke it quickly while both of us watched the road ahead and behind for any signs of traffic. It had only been two days since I had my last cigarette, so my feeling of light headedness was a little surprising.

There had been one nagging question I had since we had been sentenced and this was the last opportunity I'd have to ask it. "John, someone told me about getting remission on our sentence at Christmas. Do you know anything about that?"

John's answer was almost instantaneous. "You're right, I'd forgotten all about that! I'm not sure of the exact wording in Queen's Regulations, but the gist of it is that at Christmas the Queen often granted a remission of sentence to all commonwealth military prisoners, except for those serving time for murder, rape, and manslaughter." I felt some small glimmer of hope in the realization that Christmas was only a week away and we at least had a chance of getting an early release from jail. John and I were both smiling from ear to ear, but his next words quickly brought me back to earth. "Try not to get your hopes up too much," he said, looking serious. "Sometimes remission is granted and sometimes it's not." The chances may be slim, but at least it gave me something to hope for over the next few days. After delaying as long as we dared, John finally drove the last few hundred yards down the gravel road.

Once we turned onto the narrow access road and passed the last line of trees, we were met by a high barbwire fence that enclosed the entire area. A large sign on the main gate told us we were entering "Number One Field Detention Barracks." After John rang the buzzer, the gate was remotely opened by some unknown and unseen guard in the main building. The prison compound consisted of a huge open area with a single low-slung structure occupying most of the compound. The massive grey building was unlike anything I'd seen before. A huge circular rotunda formed the centre of the structure, with a series of six separate wings jutting out on all sides like spokes on a wheel.

Before I could even step out of the jeep, I was met by a chorus of screams from one of the waiting guards. "Get your ass in gear, boy! We haven't got all day!" By the time I could reach into the back seat to retrieve my kit bag, he was already standing with his mouth just inches from my ear. "You best move a lot faster than that, boy." With my kit bag slung over my shoulder, he marched me down the long hallway, where we finally emerged into the huge, domelike rotunda at the very centre of the building. I was sweating profusely and almost out of breath when he finally ordered me to halt. "You've got one minute to get your gear unpacked and everything laid out on the floor." In an instant, I was elbow-deep in my kit bag, trying to remove each item as quickly as possible. I thought I was moving with lighting speed, but I was obviously wrong. "Too slow, boy," he roared, shoving me out of the way. In one swift motion, he picked up my kit bag, flipped it upside down, and dumped everything in a heap on the floor. As I stood there at attention, he carefully inspected each and every item, looking for what I assumed was contraband. Nothing was left unchecked. My socks were unrolled, checked, and unceremoniously thrown across the floor. After looking inside the soap case and squeezing my toothpaste tube, each individual item in my shaving kit was dumped on the floor.

Once he was satisfied that all was in order, I was thrown two grey blankets and told to pack up my kit. Thinking he wanted me to put my belongings back in the kit bag, I immediately began stuffing things back inside as fast as I could. Once again my assumptions were incorrect. "What hell are you doing boy? Are you stupid or something?" he screamed, grabbing the blanket and flinging it on the floor. "Use that and be quick about it!" By then my head was really spinning as I ran around the floor, piling stuff into my arms, and dumping it into the middle of the blanket. Once I had everything, I immediately grabbed all four corners together and flung the improvised blanket sack over my shoulder. He paused for just a moment and just smiled. "Now you're catchin' on, boy. Who knows, given a couple of months in here, we may even be able to make you into a proper soldier."

It only took a scant second to survey the tiny cell that would make up my home for the next two weeks. It took exactly three normal paces to go from the cell door to the back wall. The only openings to the outside world were provided by a small viewing hole in the centre of the cell door and an equally small mesh wire window at the very top of the back wall. Standing in the middle of the floor, I could stretch out both arms and just about touch the grey walls on either side. My bed filled almost half the room and consisted of nothing more than a thick sheet of wood, with four metal leg supports. I assumed that the short wooden four-by-eight inch board nailed to the top on the bed was supposed to be my pillow. Other than the bed, the only other items in the cell were a bucket and a bible.

My solitude lasted less than fifteen minutes, as a different guard with the same type of bellowing voice came storming into my tiny cell. I had been sitting on the end of my wooden bed contemplation the twelve days, seven hours, and sixteen minutes I still had remaining on my sentence, and barely had time to spring to my feet when he entered. "Here, read and remember this," he snarled and threw a sheet of paper in my direction. "I'll be back shortly to check on you."

The balance of the afternoon was spent learning the multitude of rules I would have to follow:

- No talking to any of the other prisoners at any time.

- If you need to talk to one of the guards, you must first ask permission to speak.

- If you need to use the toilet, ask to speak and then ask "permission of use the facilities."

- All guards were to be addressed as "staff," regardless of their rank.

- As soon as the staff enter your cell, you must come to attention and immediately shout out your service number, last name, rank, your crime, and the length of your sentence.

- Spoons were the only utensil issued for eating.

- Shaving in the morning would be supervised by the guard, who would be the only one allowed to put a blade in your razor and remove it as soon as you were done.

- Reveille in the morning was at 5:00 a.m., and lights out was at 9:00 p.m.

- First inspection would be at 5:30 a.m. each day.

- Any fault found during inspection, however minor, would result in a charge being laid.

- If you had to go to the toilet at night, use the bucket in your cell, but it would have to be cleaned and polished before first inspection the following morning.

- All meals would be picked up from the kitchen and taken to your cell, where you would have fifteen minutes to eat before having to return your tray.

- With the exception of the fifteen-minute meals or going to bed at night, you must remain on your feet at all times when in your cell.

The rules and regulations kept coming fast and furious all afternoon. By the end of the day my head was spinning. Just when I thought I was about to drown in everything coming at me, the guard suddenly looked at his watch and rushed out of the cell, warning me to stand by for supper. He had taken back the list of rules, so I just stood there feeling very unsure about what I should do next.

I didn't have long to wait for his booming command to echo down the hallway. "Stand in your door! Step out!" He hadn't told me about this particular order, but I found myself reacting instinctively to his booming voice. I stood there in the hallway just in front of my cell, waiting for the next command. "Inwards turn!" By then I could see other prisoners out of the corner of my eye, so I just followed their lead, as they all turned in unison and began marching toward the centre rotunda.

As each person stepped to the small opening in the bars, a tray containing a plate of unrecognizable food and a mug of black coffee was shoved in their direction. Once our small band of fifteen or so prisoners all had a tray in hand, we were marched back to our cells.

To actually call what we did "marching" is a bit of a misnomer. The pace of movement, wherever we went in the detention barracks, was always somewhere between speed walking and running. Trying not to spill a tray of food and drink while marching at 120 beats to the minute is a daunting task that I never learned to master during my short stay in detention. At least the trip to return my tray was a lot easier, because, in spite of the food being bland and tasteless, I ate and drank every morsel given to me. With breakfast over twelve hours away, it didn't pay to be too fussy.

The most surprising thing I'd noted about the place was its sheer size. What struck me as odd was that we fifteen prisoners appeared to be the only inmates in a facility that was obviously designed to house at least a hundred prisoners.

After supper, any thoughts of getting even a moment's peace were shattered when yet another guard came strutting into my cell. Instead of an instruction list, this time I was handed a large black and white photo. After giving me a minute to look it over, he once again stormed out with the warning he'd be back in twenty minutes to check my work.

I quickly set about the job of laying out each item of my kit on the wooden bed, in precisely the way it was shown in the photograph. The two woollen blankets were neatly folded and placed atop my wooden pillow, with my helmet resting in the centre. Next was the web belt, containing my water bottle canteen, mess tins, and small back pack. Underneath that was laid everything from my winter grey coat, my underwear, t-shirts, and socks. There was even a designated spot for a can of Brasso, a boot brush, and a can of shoe polish. My boots and shoes sat at the very end of the bed with my bucket and bible right beside them. After fifteen minutes or so I took a step back to compare my efforts with the photo. I thought my bed layout bore a reasonable resemblance to the picture, but judging by everything littered about the cell floor after the guard finished his first inspecting, I was obviously wrong.

For the next two hours, he would return not less than four times to declare almost everything "unacceptable," as he callously threw my belongings about the cell. I was almost grateful when only half my kit found the floor on his fifth and final inspection of the night. "You have less than ten minutes until lights out. Get this mess cleaned up and get ready for bed!" I took a long, deep breath, thinking that at last I would be left alone at least for a few hours. Just before departing, he turned to take one more parting shot. "Your section staff will be inspecting tomorrow morning, and if your kit is even half as bad as what I've seen tonight, you, my dopey little friend, will find yourself in a world of hurt."

I didn't have a lot of time to ponder his threats. I had hardly started picking up the various pieces of kit from the floor, when the room went dark. It took a while for my eyes to adjust to the blackness, but using the natural light coming through the cell window and the small shaft of light from the base of the cell door, I was able to sort through the mess on the floor.

My last decision for the night was a tough one. After spending so much time getting the blankets folded correctly, I almost hated to have to take them apart for sleeping. With one blanket underneath, acting as a thin cushion against the hardwood mattress, and the other blanket pulled around me, I finally fell into a fitful sleep.

When my section staff sergeant entered my cell the next morning, nothing could have prepared me for the massive figure that filled the entire door frame. At six foot, ten inches tall and roughly 280 pounds, Sergeant Alexander was reputed to be the largest man in the entire Canadian Forces. As soon as his mountainous figure stopped in front of me, I began reciting the little speech we had been taught to regurgitate at the start of every inspection. "Staff, I am SB186 986, Private Burke T, currently serving fourteen days for conduct to the prejudice of good order and discipline, Staff!" The moment I finished, he began to speak.

"Look me in the eye, boy," he bellowed from above. It took some effort, but by craning my head straight back into my collar, I could just manage to meet his gaze. I felt a momentary sense of relief when he at last backed away and turned his attention to my bed layout. For such a big man, he certainly seemed to move with lighting speed, as he set about destroying everything I'd done that morning. My helmet was flung against the wall, followed almost immediately by both blankets. Smaller items, like socks and underwear, were just casually thrown over his shoulder in my general direction. By the time he finished, not a single article of kit remained on the bed. After kicking some kit aside, he once again stood before me. "Sonny, boy," he said, "you are one sorry sack of shit." After a moment's pause, he went on. "I'll give you one more day to get your shit together, but if I don't see an improvement tomorrow, you and I are going to pay a little visit to the commandant."

Later that afternoon I was busy trying to buff the dull stains from my mess tins with a piece of steel wool. Getting some kind of shine from the dull metal was hard, mind-numbing work, but slowly a slight lustre began to appear. With the exception of the quick trip to pick up and return lunch, I had been cleaning, ironing, and shining since early morning. If nothing else, at least it kept my mind somewhat occupied and not craving a cigarette every few minutes.

Sometime in the late afternoon I heard Paddy's familiar voice asking for permission to use the toilet. I'm sure I wasn't the first and I definitely wouldn't be the last one to figure out that if you wanted to talk to somebody, asking to use the toilet would be the one and only opportunity to do it. It was difficult to tell without a watch, but after what I estimated to be about three minutes, I took a deep breath and yelled to the guard in the distant rotunda.

Even though it had been just three days and we could only speak in whispers for less than a minute, it was good at least to hear a friendly voice. Paddy was his normal calm self, but even he jumped when we thought we heard the guard's footsteps coming down the corridor. When I told him about my preparations for the next inspection, he just smiled and told me not to waste my time. "Don't you get it?" he said. "It really doesn't matter what you do, you're going to be charged at least once, maybe twice."

It may have been hopeless, but that didn't stop me from at least trying to have an absolutely perfect kit layout for the Monday morning inspection. Regardless of my efforts, it took Sergeant Alexander about ten seconds to find a fault. After swiping his fingers over the edge of my wooden pillow, he held his outstretched hand in front of my face. "See that boy! That's dust from your bed. Consider yourself on charge!"

Based on the speed with which I was brought before the commandant, I am sure they must have had the charge report draw up and ready to go. With practically every prisoner being charged almost every day, I assumed they had forms prepared for all contingencies. All they would have to do is fill in the blanks with the appropriate name and add the phrase "dirty" or "dusty" or perhaps "filthy" and they were ready to go.

My entire trial took less than five minutes. "You are charged with an act to the prejudice and good order, in that your bed was dusty. Do you have anything to say for yourself, Private?" The prison commandant had not even bothered to look at me since I'd been marched into his office.

"No sir, I have nothing to say." He at last looked up at me for just a moment, before pronouncing sentence.

"I find you guilty, and award you three days bread and water."

I wasn't surprised by the sentence. Paddy and Zeke had already completed the identical sentence on their first charge. As I was marched out of the commandant's office, both of them were just being lined up to go in for their second trial. Everything had happened so fast, I hardly had time to feel nervous. Even later when the guard explained exactly what my sentence entailed, I just calmly stood there listening, but not caring what he had to say.

"You have been awarded three days bread and water, which means you will report to the kitchen each morning and receive six slices of bread and one canteen of water. When you eat it is up to you, but that's all you will get for each day's ration."

By the end of day two I was absolutely famished and feeling slightly light-headed. The daily routine had become quite familiar to me. Each morning the prisoners were taken outside for an hour for what the guards euphemistically called "recreation." At precisely eleven o'clock in the morning, the command to don your equipment and stand in your door would echo down the hallway. Once the prisoners were lined up in the centre of the corridor, they would be marched out to the parade square for close order drill. This recreation, as the guards called it, entailed a solid hour of nonstop drill at 120 paces to the minute, while wearing a helmet, web belt, and large backpack. It sounds silly now, but at the time I actually looked forward to these mornings of drill. In spite of the strenuous nature of the drill, at least we were outside in the fresh air.

As supper time approached on my last day of bread and water, I was absolutely ravenous, but I had concocted a little plan that, if timed just right, could get me just a little more food.

Not surprisingly, Paddy and Zeke had already been found guilty of their second crime. Whether it was dust on their bed, a missed whisker while shaving, or perhaps a fingerprint on their brass buckle, I really don't know. Both had been sentenced to forty eight hours in the "hole" for whatever horrendous crime they had committed.

The "hole" was just a few small, windowless cells near the end of the corridor. The punishment was really quite simple. The prisoner was locked in one of these cells with nothing but a bible, bucket, and a single grey flannel blanket. He could keep his coveralls and boots, but the laces were removed. The cell was kept in constant darkness and the prisoner could not leave for the duration of his sentence. Although I understood the need for the bucket, because the prisoner would eventually have to answer the call of nature, it was never clear to me why he would need a bible. Perhaps our jailers believed that its very presence could bring some measure of comfort to the cell's occupant.

Hours of just sitting alone in the darkness can seem endless, but there was at least the tiniest of breaks at meal times each day. Prisoners sentenced to the "hole" were still entitled to regular meals, but because they were not allowed out of their confinement, someone had to bring their tray of food to them.

In this case, I was the perfect delivery boy. Being on bread and water, I was free to carry trays back and forth from the kitchen. The plan was simple, but my timing would have to be perfect or I could find myself in a dark cell for the balance of my sentence. After delivering the supper meal to the guys, I sat back in my own cell slowly chewing on a slice of dry bread and patiently waiting for the call to pick up the empty trays.

As luck would have it, my escort guard stayed in front of me as I moved down the hall, holding the almost empty tray in my outstretched arms. A small scoop of leftover potatoes and mixed vegetables just sat there, right in the middle of the plate, waiting to be taken. After a fugitive glance to ensure my escort wasn't looking, I quickly raised the tray straight up to my open mouth, and in one gulp I managed to ingest all of the remains. My biggest fear was missing the target and being caught for leaving some tiny particle around my mouth. I didn't have a free hand, but after some delicate manoeuvring, I was able to wipe away any evidence on the upper arm of my coveralls.

It wasn't much and it certainly didn't stop the pangs of hunger, but later on in my cell I almost burst into laughter. It just felt so good to have put something over on these people who were trying to starve me into submission.

On Christmas Eve, Zeke and I were both allowed into the main rotunda to do a little ironing. Ever since Paddy and I had our first bathroom conversation, I had been worried about Zeke. He and I had never had the chance to speak, but based upon the strained look on his face the first day I saw him, I knew he wasn't coping well. He appeared to be a man at the very edge of a nervous breakdown. When the guard made some remark to him about his ironing, he practically knocked over the table when he jumped to attention to answer the question.

My eyes were wide open long before the guard came banging on the cell doors at 5:30 a.m. on Christmas morning. Absolutely nothing had been said about any remission of our sentences, but I somehow believed there was some chance but if it was going to happen it had to be then. I thought there was some small ray of hope when the guard came around and announced there would be no inspection that morning. After a breakfast of the standard lumpy porridge and black coffee, you could almost feel the anticipation of everyone sitting in their cells, waiting to for something to happen. After a long morning of uninterrupted work in our cells, even I had pretty much given up hope of being granted a reprieve.

Just before eleven, the guard's booming voice filled the hallway. "Stand in your door! Step out!" I knew this was the normal time for drill, but we hadn't been told to don our equipment, which was rather odd. Once we were all lined up in the corridor, there was a long pause as we all just stood there apprehensively waiting his next command. Finally he spoke. "Because it's a holiday, you people are going to get a little break." We all strained forward, anticipating his next words. *Oh my God,* I thought, *they're going to let us out of here early!*

"We will be doing drill without packs today." Judging by his wide grin, I'm sure he thought he was doing us a real favour, but when he saw the dead-pan expressions on our faces his smile quickly disappeared. "Right then, let's get on with it. Merry Christmas — quick march!"

By the time we came back inside at noon, any glimmer of hope I may have had about remission was long gone. All I was hoping for was the chance to finally stop just long enough to catch my breath. Even though we were back inside the building, the speedy pace continued. Normally when we reached the area in front of our cells, we would be halted and told to fall out and prepare for lunch. For the second time today, things were different as we continued marching up the hall and into the main rotunda.

After a short pause to let us catch our breath, the guard finally spoke. "Right, gents. In spite of your slovenly drill performance this morning, I have decided to give you all a little break today. You will have your lunch together, over there," he said, pointing at a long table set up next to the kitchen. "You have one hour in which you can talk."

One would think that since we had permission to speak the non-stop chatter would have started immediately, but strangely enough we all just sat there, dumbly looking around. It was like everyone was waiting for someone else to break the awkward silence. It started very slowly, but finally one brave soul at the end of the table broke the ice. "Well, will you look at that!" he pointed excitedly at the pack of cigarettes sitting in the middle of the table.

Within moments, the flood gates were open and everyone started talking at once. Zeke seemed to be silent the longest. At first he just sat there expressionless and staring at the food on his plate. I wasn't the only one who had noticed the subtle changes in Zeke's personality. It took quite a while, but finally he began to smile and utter a few words. By the end of the hour, he was as animated and talkative as the rest of us. I could see the guard looking at his watch, and we all knew we were only a few minutes away from returning to our enforced silence.

"Right, gents, you have five minutes to finish up," our guard warned. Almost immediately, everyone sprung into action. Some were trying to smoke two cigarettes at once, while others attempted to shovel every last morsel of remaining food down their throats. Just before we were ordered back to our cells I at least managed to get a smile out of Zeke by reminding him that we had only five days left before our release.

• • •

My ability to dodge a second charge had absolutely nothing to do with my almost picture perfect kit layout each morning. The slight delay in my arrival time had simply allowed me to enter detention just as the holidays were about to start. Any thoughts I may have had about getting through my sentence without suffering any further damage were brought to a crushing halt shortly after Christmas.

Not surprisingly, the holidays had not mellowed Staff Alexander in the least. The second he came through the door and stepped in front of me, he found the egregious fault that would put me in the hole for two days.

It had been a particularly warm and stuffy morning, and I scurried about the cell, trying to put the last touches on my kit before the inspection began. I was sweating profusely under my heavy coveralls and honestly don't remember undoing my top button. "Do you think this is some kind of a holiday resort, Burke? You look like a sack of shit, tied in the middle!" At this point I had no idea what he was talking about. The fact that I just stood there looking dumbly ahead only served to make him angrier. "Coveralls must be done up to the neck at all times! Consider yourself on charge for being improperly dressed!"

It is simply unimaginable how long it can take for forty-eight hours to pass when you are left sitting alone in a dark, windowless cell. By dinner on the second day, I wasn't hungry at all, so I decided to get a little creative with my food.

The hamburger patty was rather small, but I had managed to dig a hole right in the centre. I then took the minuscule portion of peas and carrots and jammed them firmly into the hole. The remaining mash potatoes were then arranged in a tight circle around the patty. I must say that when I caught a momentary glance of my work in the light in the door slot, I was quite pleased with my effort. The potato and brown meat patty formed the outer and inner rings of my little target. The squashed peas and carrots, at the very centre were meant to form a bull's eye, which I could only hope the prisoner saw and had the opportunity to attack. I know now that my actions might be seen as borderline lunacy, but, at the time, I could only smile and feel somewhat happy in my tiny act of rebellion.

• • •

December 31, our day of freedom, finally arrived. Sergeant Alexander was almost cordial while he carried out our final morning inspection. By then I knew my kit was just about perfect, but still he managed to litter the floor with most of my belongings.

As usual when our morning period of close quarter drill ended, we were all completely out of breath. Even though I could only see the back of Zeke's head, I knew instinctively that, like me, he was smiling from ear to ear. We were done. All that remained was to be marched back inside, pack up our kit, and be marched out the front door.

Just as our little group approached the edge of the parade square, our drill instructor's voice came echoing from the rear. "Prisoners, halt!" The combination of a surprise order and the slippery asphalt caused some minor collisions as each of us tried to stop.

I could hear the footsteps of our instructor coming up behind me, and after a moment I could feel his warm breath while he stood just inches away. "Burke, the buckle on your pack is a disgrace." His words were delivered in a low, threatening tone. My friend Zeke was the next in line, and his brass was also found to be dirty. After passing four more prisoners without comment, he reached Paddy and uttered just two words: "Dirty brass."

Not surprisingly, the only people he found fault with were the three scheduled for release that very morning. How strange it was that we all had exactly the same faulty brass.

I have to admit his next words did manage to scare me a little. "I know you three morons are due for release at noon, but that can be easily postponed. This being New Year's Eve, most of the staff will be going home early, so if your release paperwork is not signed soon, it will have to wait until the commandant returns, on January 2." We all listened intently, not knowing if he was speaking the truth or just pulling one last cruel joke on three helpless prisoners. "You've got thirty minutes to shine those buckles or you will find yourselves here for an extra three days!"

I swear there were sparks flying off that piece of steel wool as I madly attacked each buckle on my back pack. After about ten minutes all three of us were standing in the rotunda, anxiously waiting for our work to be checked. With barely a glance, our tormentor picked up and threw the packs at us in disgust. "This is absolute crap! Do it again." As we hurried back to our cells, his threatening shouts followed us. "You best get a move on! The commandant will be leaving soon and you know what that means."

After I got back to my cell, I just threw my pack down in disgust and stood there doing nothing. Either he was bluffing or we would remain incarcerated for a few more days. Just minutes before noon we were once more called from our cells. "You three clowns get your asses up here right now!" Zeke and I almost crashed into each other in our effort to get to the rotunda. Again, the guard grabbed the packs from our outstretched arms. After a cursory glance at the buckles, he threw our packs back at us. "Now that's much better. Your ride is waiting outside," he said, tapping his watch. "You have exactly five minutes to get your sorry asses out of my prison."

• • •

After missing out on Christmas completely, I had spent the last week in prison thinking of all the things I was going to do when I got out on New Year's Eve. My first order of business would be to devour an entire chicken at Lucy's Gasthof. That would be followed by a few gallons of beer at the Candlelight Bar in Soest. By midnight I planned to be among the many drunks at the Copacabana.

As the saying goes, "the best laid plans often go asunder." After an unhurried shower back in the quarters, I thought I'd take a quick nap before heading out.

At first I was a bit startled and disoriented, when I woke up at five o'clock the next morning and realized I missed the entire night, but once I realized there was nobody screaming for me to get ready for inspection, I just smiled thankfully to myself, rolled over, and went back to sleep.

Chapter 11
Dating in Sign Language

I have to admit that when I was first told what we were about to do, I had grave doubts in my ability to actually pull it off. I think most of the guys in pioneer platoon were a little surprised by the announcement, but as I looked around our little group, the majority looked self assured. *Easy for them,* I thought. *I'm barely nineteen and most of these guys have a good eight to ten years on me.*

I could still clearly remember the very first morning's inspection during basic training, where I had been picked up for having some minute patches of peach fuzz on my baby face. But there I was, barely twenty months later, and I was being told I had to grow a full beard.

The hundred-year-old practice of pioneers wearing scarlet uniforms and full beards for ceremonial parades had been one of many traditions carried over from the British Army. Just after getting to the platoon I had been fitted for the full uniform. As I stood there in front of the mirror, I have to admit I looked quite smart. The white leather apron fit snugly on top of the scarlet tunic. With the spiked pith helmet sitting squarely on my head and the chrome-plated axe glistening brightly on my shoulder, the outfit was almost complete. All that was missing was facial hair.

I need not have worried. My beard may have been various shades of brown, but it was at least an even growth in all the right places. When the regimental sergeant major arrived to check our progress some two months later, he took less than five minutes to decide our fate. We all stood shoulder to shoulder while he quickly passed in front of each man and made his pronouncement. For those with patchy bald spots or thin, sporadic growth the words were: "shave it off." For those of us with a full growth, the three words were equally simple: "keep it on."

When the day of the big parade finally arrived on that exceptionally hot July afternoon, I was absolutely soaked in sweat from the heavy flannel uniform and leather apron we wore. I could feel the tiny rivets of sweat dripping through my beard and slowly making their way under the collar of my scarlet tunic.

We had weeks of rehearsals for what was to be a huge parade, celebrating Canada's one-hundredth birthday. The spectacle would begin with an artillery gun salute from the 105mm Howitzers lined up right beside us, at the very edge of the parade square. Once the last gun fired, we six pioneers would lead the entire parade into the square. Immediately behind us was the commanding officer, followed by the corps of drums and the eight hundred men of the battalion.

In my scarlet uniform with axe and beard, on July 1, 1967.

From my vantage point at the very front of the parade, I could see that almost everything was unfolding precisely as it had been rehearsed. The one key exception was the line of 105mm field guns that started just ten feet to the right of my position. During all the rehearsals the artillery crews had only gone through dry drills, but now the guns would fire one hundred blank rounds to signify the start of the parade.

I'm not sure exactly when, but somewhere around the seventieth or eightieth explosion I began to hear a low ringing in my ears. By the time the guns finally ended their one-hundred gun salute, the only sound I could hear was the even increasing ringing noise and nothing else.

We were scant seconds away from receiving the colonel's command to march on, so I had to act fast. "Can you hear me?" I was trying to whisper to the man on my left, but I had no idea how loud I was speaking. "Give me a poke in the ribs when the CO starts." I had no idea if this would work, but I hardly had time to think about it before feeling the sudden jolt of an elbow striking my rib cage. Almost instantaneously, my left foot shot forward and we were off across the parade square.

It took a couple of days for the ringing in my ears to finally disappear. After the parade I fully expected to be called on the carpet over my obviously poor drill, but I soon discovered that there were many people, including the colonel, who experienced the same short-term hearing loss.

With all the emphasis on the Canada Day parade, almost the entire spring training schedule was thrown out of whack. The ten-mile battle fitness test was cancelled completely, but considering all the weeks spent pounding the drill square, we probably covered a good deal more ground. Because the normal work up exercise in Haltern was also cancelled, we would cover the missed training by spending an extra week in Sennelager.

By the time we reached Sennelager in mid August, the novelty of having a full beard had completely worn off. Those first few weeks in July, while we were still living in the barracks, our morning routine was quick and simple. It is easy enough to maintain a good level of cleanliness when sinks and showers are readily available, but after only a few hours of running around in the heat and dust of Sennelager, the itching and scratching soon began.

Despite my best efforts to keep it clean, by the last week of the exercise my entire neck was covered in a solid red rash. Sergeant Stoke's announcement that we would be removing our beards as soon as we returned to Fort York was met with a collective sigh of relief.

The plan was simple. Each man would be given an appointment at the barber shop on our first day back. Unfortunately, any thoughts we may of had about having our facial hair comfortably removed by a professional were completely dashed when our clean-shaven young platoon commander showed up for morning parade on our second to last day in Sennelager.

Apparently after getting very drunk and passing out in the officer's mess tent the night before, some of his officer friends had shaved off his beard while he lay there. After a moment of debate with the platoon sergeant, the decision was made. It would not be fitting for our leader to stand before us with skin as hairless as a baby's behind while we all still stood there still looking like scruffy lumberjacks.

It took most of the morning, but with the use of some tiny scissors found in the first aid kit, a side mirror from a truck, a few basins of lukewarm water, and a good number of razor blades, the job was finally done. It took every available band aid and a half roll of toilet paper to cover the numerous cuts and stop the bleeding, but by noon our naked faces were once again back at work.

• • •

By the time the final fall exercise was over in late September, you could almost feel the collective sense of fatigue throughout the battalion. The weather had been particularly nasty for the last week of the exercise, and by the time we finally boarded the train for the long ride home, tempers were short. The usual noise and laughter found at the end of a long, hard exercise was completely absent. The grey sky and pelting rain outside seemed to match the mood inside the train.

For the former members of Hill 70 Platoon, the fall of 1967 was a time of decision. Our initial three-year contract with the military was about to expire, which meant that each of us had just weeks to decide whether to leave for home or reenlist for another three-year tour of duty.

For some, like me, the decision was easy. After all, my family situation back in Canada had not changed. Although I still maintained some written contact with my brothers and sisters, I no longer felt part of that life. In spite of any minor trials and tribulations, I had absolutely no intention of returning to civilian life anytime soon.

On the last day in September, the twenty or so members of our former platoon met in the Red Patch Club for what for many would be our final farewell drink. The evening started out quiet enough, but, as usual, when liquor was involved the party soon became a loud and raucous affair. By ten o'clock the bartender had manoeuvred us all into the games room, where he quickly closed the sliding doors in an effort to shield his other customers.

Everywhere I looked that night I could see nothing but smiling faces. It was sad to think that within a week or two only about half of the original group would remain, but at least everyone was happily enjoying this last gathering. No doubt, that night there were many heartfelt promises made to stay in touch, but I think we all knew the truth. Sure, we would get the odd postcard telling us that one of our friends had made it home safely, but in the vast majority of cases, within a few weeks or months all contact would be lost forever.

• • •

It had been a long exhausting summer and fall, but finally, in early October, the colonel announced that everyone would receive a four-day long weekend for all their hard work. Almost as if by magic, the sombre mood of the battalion was finally lifted.

By supper time on Thursday evening, the base was practically deserted. Most of my friends had already departed for Amsterdam, but I just felt the urge to stay in camp and have a quiet weekend. Paddy and I had been back to Amsterdam twice since our little incident, so the prospect of running into our friends at the border no longer worried me.

I was almost sorry to see Monday afternoon roll around. The shack had been so peaceful and quiet the entire long weekend, but I knew that was about to change. Any thought I may have had about my last few hours of peace was quickly erased when two of my friends came barging through the front door. They may not have been completely drunk, but were certainly well on their way when they came shouting and stumbling toward my bed space.

From the day Bob Stuckless and I had snuck out of the shack and gone drinking in downtown London, we had become fast friends. How could you not like someone so boisterous and so full of life? He had always been a straight-forward, easy-going guy, but these past few months has been the happiest I'd ever seen him. He had met German girl months earlier and they planned to get married in the coming year.

Paul Currie had come through basic training with us, but I only really got to know him as a friend after we arrived in Germany. Paul was a tall, good-looking

French Canadian with an infectious smile. His huge, bellowing laugh could fill an entire room.

"Come on, get dressed. We're taking you out for a few beers." I tried making excuses about being tired, but they weren't buying it. "Bullshit man, this is your day and we're going out to celebrate!" Paul just sat there on the end of the bed, smiling and refusing to move. I tried to pretend I was upset as I got dressed, but deep down I was actually quite happy that someone had actually remembered it was my twentieth birthday.

I don't necessarily believe that there is some grand design to life. Maybe there is a purpose to everything, or perhaps it is all just random chance. At the ripe old age of twenty, I certainly didn't give much thought to such heady questions. But, as the years passed, the thought has often crossed my mind that perhaps I was meant to get in that taxi with those guys and head downtown on that very night. One thing I know for sure, had I talked my way out of going, my life would most likely be very different today.

By the time we reached the downtown core, we quickly realized we had made a gross miscalculation. It didn't dawn on any of us until we actually stopped in front of the Candlelight Bar and found it locked up tight. It was a Monday, which meant that almost all our regular haunts were closed for business.

Earlier I hadn't wanted to go out at all, but now that we were actually downtown, I just didn't want to give up. Seeing the look of dejection on our faces, our taxi driver suggested we try a place he knew at the very edge of the old city.

The Sanrimo Restaurant was a newer place, situated right up against the ancient city wall. I had passed the place once or twice, but never given it a second thought. Paul said he'd been there once and although the food was good, the clientele was almost exclusively German.

The place was quite full, but no one gave us more than a cursory glance as we made our way through the crowd to the few free stools at the end of the bar. By the time we finished our second round of beer, we had all but forgotten our earlier difficulties. We were actually having a good time trying out our extremely limited German language skills on the bartender. I could see Paul was getting quite drunk, and I thought a little food might slow him down.

We had just moved to a table to eat when I saw her for the very first time. I just sat there staring at what I believed to be the best-looking German woman I had ever seen. After a few moments I could see I was making her uncomfortable, so I forced myself to look away.

"Cutlet und fritten," Paul said, pointing hopefully at the menu. It was obvious that our waitress didn't speak a word of English, but after a momentary glance at the menu, she just smiled and nodded her head. Not wanting to make things any more difficult on our nervous waitress, Bob and I ordered the same veal cutlet and french fries.

When the food arrived twenty minutes later, Paul was already quite drunk and more than a little agitated. Judging by the speed with which she placed the plates of food in front of us, I knew she was a little unnerved by my constant staring. In a flash she was heading for the safety of the kitchen.

Both of the guys had been far more interested in devouring their food and took no notice of me, as I twisted around in my seat, trying to keep my eyes on our waitress. She was just steps away from disappearing through the swinging door, when Paul called out to her.

"Nix good, no good," he kept repeating, as he pointed at his cutlet. The poor girl obviously didn't comprehend what Paul was getting at, as he continued to jab his knife at the meat on his plate. Paul was trying to tell her that his cutlet was undercooked, but she was obviously having a difficult time trying to understand his drunken mixture of French, German, and English. Paul's voice was becoming louder, as his continued efforts to explain were met with only blank stares from our pretty waitress. It can't have been easy standing there listening to some rude and drunken foreigner shouting at you over god knows what.

When Paul finally grabbed the cutlet off his plate and shoved it toward her, she quickly backed away and began crying, and she ran back into the kitchen. The words were right on the tip of my tongue, but before I could say anything Bob came out with exactly what I was thinking. "You know Paul, you truly are an asshole." Paul just sat there looking defiant, as he still held the partly eaten cutlet in his hand. I honestly don't know where I found the courage, but once I saw that Paul was unmoving, I got up without a word and headed toward the kitchen.

To say women frightened me would be an understatement. It may have been my Catholic upbringing, or perhaps it had to do with attending boys only schools in Ireland and Canada — I really don't know. Whatever the reason, the fact was that the prospect of dealing with most women in a social situation simply scared the hell out of me. Sure I'd been with a few girls before leaving Canada, and certainly had no difficulty dealing with women in Soest or Amsterdam, but these women can best be described as "being of loose virtue." I was not naïve enough to believe that that the females who populated the canal district of Amsterdam where interested in anything other than my money. When one of these girls invited herself to your table in the Derby Bar, she wasn't there to listen to your enthralling conversation. Their interest in you lasted only as long as the free drinks kept coming.

As I walked through the kitchen door, I had absolutely no idea what I should say, but I knew I had to act quickly before I lost my nerve. This would have been difficult enough to do in English, but there I was, about to try and apologize for the behaviour of someone else and my total German vocabulary consisted of perhaps ten words.

Thankfully by then she had stopped crying, but based on the angry look she gave me, I knew she wasn't in a very forgiving mood. At first it felt like I was talking to a stone wall while she continued to glare at me. I only wished I knew the German words for "sorry" or "apologize," but I didn't so I just pressed on in broken English. Very slowly her facial muscles relaxed. She obviously didn't understand my words, but I think she was beginning to grasp my meaning.

I don't know how long it took Paul to realize just how big a favour he had done me. Had he acted like a normal person we probably would have eaten our meal and left, never to return. Because of his rude behaviour I had been given an opportunity to do something I might otherwise never have done.

It took about twenty more visits to the Sanrimo Restaurant and more than a little help from her English-speaking boss, but finally she agreed to go out with me. Dating in sign language is never easy, but somehow we managed to keep it going. By the end of the sixth month together I had taken enough classes in German to have somewhat of a normal conversation without the aid of a translator.

Barely thirteen months after we met, we were married.

After a simple ceremony, our little wedding party headed for the Red Patch for a small celebration. My friend Bob Stuckless had gotten married a couple of months earlier and was only too happy to share with me all the wisdom he gained from his sixty days of marriage experience.

Thankfully Paul remained relatively sober throughout the evening. After some initial awkwardness, he and Brigitte had become friends. She may not have understood much English, but even Brigitte found it funny when Paul got up to make a long winded toast, in which he took full credit for bringing us two together in the first place.

By early evening our little wedding reception had turned into a wall of noise. Everywhere I looked around the massive circular table, I could see people caught up in various loud conversations. Whenever I glanced over at Brigitte, I could see she was enjoying herself in spite of the language barrier. She would sit there smiling, while another of my friends would be nattering away to her in English, completely oblivious of the fact that she probably only understood every tenth word.

Sadly the one Canadian she called her friend and protector was missing from that all-important day.

The very first time I brought Brigitte to the Red Patch, I had introduced her to Alvin Morris and they became almost instant friends. Although his first name was Alvin, almost everybody referred to him as Moose. At well over six feet tall and weighing a solid 230 pounds, he was certainly an imposing figure. He was only in his mid twenties, but the deep-set lines on his face and his ruddy complexion gave the impression of someone much older. At first glance Moose may have seemed intimidating, but once he smiled with that huge toothy grin you knew there was nothing to fear.

On one occasion shortly after Brigitte and I began dating, I was late arriving for our meeting in front of Dicka Willy's Restaurant. While she waited for me to arrive, two drunken Germans had tried to pick her up. After repeated requests to leave her alone, the two persisted in harassing her. She was becoming a little frantic when, to her great relief, she spotted Moose getting out of a taxi in front of the Candlelight Bar. It had taken Moose just seconds to assess the situation, and I'm sure that before they even realized what was happening both Germans were pinned firmly against the wall. Just as they were both about to pass out from fright, Brigitte convinced Moose to let them go. Drunk or not, they both beat a hasty retreat.

By the time I showed up to find her sitting alone in a corner booth, everything was long over. Brigitte had not wanted to sit waiting alone in the middle of a restaurant, but Moose refused to leave unless she went inside.

Had Moose not reappeared later, I probably would never have known anything about what had happened. When I tried thanking him, Moose would hear nothing of it. "You have a good woman there, Stoney. Just make sure you take good care of her," was all he would say.

One evening around closing time at the Candlelight, Moose and an American soldier got in an argument over a taxi. Apparently both had called for a cab, but only one showed up. After a few minutes of loud confrontation, with neither man backing down, the much smaller American invited Moose outside. As one eyewitness told me later, "Everyone thought it was ridiculous.

Moose was at least twice the size of the Yank. The fight would be absolutely no contest."

The American went out first, with Moose right behind him. As soon as both of them reached the sidewalk, the American pulled a pistol from his pocket, jabbed it into Moose's chest, and fired one shot straight through his heart. In less than a minute, Moose lay dead on the sidewalk.

It had been just over four months since Moose had died, but as we all sat there that evening in the Red Patch celebrating our wedding, it was hard not to think of our missing friend. We knew nothing would ever bring him back, but at least there we could find some solace in knowing that the American was serving twenty years of hard labour in Leavenworth Penitentiary.

That first year of marriage in Germany may have been the roughest, but it certainly was the happiest. Our tiny two-room flat had only one cold water tap. When our daughter Martina came along, it would take an hour or more to heat water on the coal stove in order to give her a bath. The only bathroom was downstairs and was shared with the landlord. In winter, our baby girl was never without at least three layers of clothes to protect her from the damp, cold wind that came whistling through every crack in the paper-thin walls.

At last I could say that for the first time in many years I actually had a good Christmas. There may have only been enough money to buy presents for the baby, and our Christmas tree was small enough to sit on a corner table, but none of that mattered because we were together.

Chapter 12
Good Luck, or Good Leadership?

If a collision with the oncoming squad was to be avoided on my first attempt at being a drill instructor, I had to do something, and I had to do it fast. It may have been the middle of January, but I was sweating profusely. My mouth was open, but the words weren't there. *For God's sake, say something!* I screamed to myself. With just two paces remaining before the squad reached the ditch at the edge of the parade square, the word of command finally came to me. "About turn!" I commanded. With less than a foot to spare, the ten-man squad executed the 180 degree turn in perfect unison.

I had been on the pre-junior NCO course for just over a week, and so far things had not gone that well. On day one of the course, I had certainly felt very enthusiastic about the prospect of becoming a corporal. After all, I had spent the past three years listening to classroom lessons and pounding out mile after mile of foot drill on the parade square. How hard could it be to actually teach this stuff? It would only take a couple of days to find out how truly naïve I really was.

The purpose of this pre-course was to select the best candidates from our battalion to attend the actual course. It was made very clear to us on day one that although there were fifty of us sitting there listening to the opening address, only the top twenty would be selected to go on the full eight week course at the brigade battle school.

After a week of intensive instruction on how to present a forty-minute classroom lecture and a drill lesson, we would be assigned a period of each to deliver to the other ten candidates in our squad.

I was somewhat relieved when I was assigned my first lesson: stripping and assembling the FN C1 rifle. Counting back to the day I joined, I had probably taken my rifle apart and put it back together at least a thousand times. This would be easy — or so I thought.

That entire middle weekend of the course was spent poring over my notes and preparing my lesson plan. Unlike school, I found the military method of instruction quite rigid, but very straightforward. All lessons, regardless of the subject, are divided into three distinct parts: the introduction, the body, and the conclusion.

The body of the lesson is where you get down to the actual nuts and bolts of teaching the material. We were given a simple but effective three-word rule to follow: "Explanation, Demonstration, Imitation." In the case of stripping the rifle, you *explain* what you are doing as you remove each piece. Next you *demonstrate* exactly how each part is removed. Once the students have seen you do it, they simply *imitate* what you have done by removing the same part from their own weapon. When the entire weapon is stripped, the exact same procedure is used to reassemble the weapon.

It certainly sounded simple enough, and by Sunday afternoon I had my lesson plan written down and I had run through numerous dry practices in front of the bathroom mirror.

I think my confidence started to wane after sitting through the first two candidate lessons on Monday morning. It was obvious that the first man up did not have a good grasp of the material. Throughout the forty minutes, he rarely made eye contact with his students and he read continually from his lesson plan. From the back of the room, I heard a distinct groan coming from our instructor as he sat assessing the lecture. At the end of thirty minutes, the instructor ended the lesson early by giving the guy a failing grade.

The second man up did marginally better. He did know his material, but his dull monotone delivery was almost too painful to bear, as he droned on for the full forty minutes. I think even he was surprised when the instructor gave him a passing grade of C–.

Almost as soon as I started talking, I could feel the beads of sweat forming on my neck and forehead. There they were, just sitting there waiting for me to speak. I don't know how or why, but suddenly I felt a wave of nervous intimidation flowing over me. It was as if a giant hand had reached into my brain and scooped out every single bit of information I'd studied and practiced that weekend. I knew I had to come out and stand in front of the class, but somehow I couldn't release my hands from their death grip on the lecture podium. I could feel the blood rushing to my head as I tried to stutter my way through the lesson introduction.

Everything was a bit of a blur after that. I tried in vain to calm down and just follow the lesson plan. I had absolutely no comprehension of time as I continued to stumble on. I felt a great sense of relief when I finally heard myself say the concluding sentence. "Today we have covered the stripping and assembly of the rifle. Are there any questions?"

I had been standing there, nervously hanging onto the podium for a full five minutes before the instructor finally stopped writing on the assessment form and made his way toward the front of the class. The expression on his face told me all I needed to know.

He didn't waste any time getting to the point. "Burke, I'm sure the guys really appreciate you wrapping up in just twenty minutes, but unfortunately you left out about half the lesson." He continued for a few minutes more, as he covered each of my faults in detail. Finally near the end he made a few positive comments about my good speaking voice and sound questioning technique. It wasn't much, but at least I had some tiny glimmer of hope that maybe next time I could do better.

Many of us "failures" talked into the night. I was gratified to hear that I wasn't alone in my nervousness. Most of the guys had fallen victim to the same thing. Like me, they knew the material, but when it came time to speak in front of an audience of their peers their nerves had failed them.

I remember reading some years later that one of the major universities in the United States had done a study to determine what people feared the most. According to their findings, better than 30 percent of the study participants ranked speaking in public as their number one fear. The remaining 70 percent picked death as their single greatest fear. I have to admit that I find it funny to think that there are a significant percentage of people who would choose to be in the coffin at a funeral, rather than delivering the eulogy.

When my time came around again, I was more than ready. The night before my second lesson about eight of us "Nervous Nellies" had gotten together in the quarters and practiced our lessons, using each other as a live audience. Our instructor looked a little stunned by the noticeable improvement, but I was more than happy to receive a solid *C+* pass.

Although the same basic rules of instruction applied equally to drill, you could no longer stand there reading from a prepared lesson plan. To succeed at drill you better have memorized the entire lesson and be ready to deliver your commands in a loud, booming voice.

Personally I found this process much easier than working in a classroom. No longer did I have to standing there staring into their faces. Everything and everyone was in motion while I shouted drill commands and watched the squad instantly react to my words.

It hadn't been a perfect period of drill, but I did manage to pass, in spite of almost marching my squad into a ditch and narrowly avoiding a head on collision with two other squads.

When the list was finally published on the last day of the pre-course, I was almost afraid to look. I watched as person after person stepped up to the notice board and slowly ran their finger down the column of names. Some found their names quickly and shouted in instant relief. Others repeatedly scanned the page from top to bottom and just walked away with a look of total dejection. I watched as my friend Bob Stuckless took his turn in front of the board. It took him a few moments, but when he stepped away I was glad to see him smiling. Before I could get to the board, Bob stepped in front of me and stuck out his hand. "Congratulations, buddy," he said, still smiling from ear to ear. "We've both made it!"

My name may have been closer to the bottom than the top of the list, but I really didn't care. I was just happy to make the cut. After all, I would have eight weeks to prove to those who choose me that I deserved to be there.

• • •

Those first couple of weeks felt like being back in basic training. If you were lucky you could manage to squeeze in a ten minute breakfast at seven o'clock, but that only left you a half hour to get ready for the most thorough inspection imaginable.

Usually by 7:30 my three roommates and I would be standing ankle deep in bedding and kit, all strung about the room by our inspecting officer. At eight o'clock sharp, the breakneck pace of training would begin. On a good day we would finish formal training by dark, but preparations for the next day kept us busy long into the night.

The last three weeks of the course were spent almost exclusively in the field. The whole purpose of this course was to teach and assess our leadership ability. If we were to successfully pass this course, we first had to prove that we could react to any situation and lead men, even when faced with extreme stress. The army's way of achieving the necessary stress level may not have been very scientific, but it certainly worked.

To test performance under extreme duress, all they had to do was keep a man awake and moving for days on end, with little or no food, and place him in command while under fire from the enemy. Add the bitter cold of a late

February day, and you quickly learn who has the right stuff. Those who folded under the pressure were usually taken from the field and sent home the same day.

As dawn broke each morning, we would all stand on alert in our trenches, waiting for the enemy to attack our position. As soon as the sun peeked over the horizon, we would once again be on the move. As long as there was daylight, we continued to advance on foot. Every few hundred yards you could count on the enemy opening fire, causing us to dive for cover in the ditch at the side of the road. Once orders were passed, we would be off and running in a mad dash to a flanking position, ready to attack. Amid the noise of machinegun fire, the haze of smoke grenades, and the constant yelling of our candidate commander, we would gallop forward, overrunning the enemy before consolidating on the other side. After a hasty check on ammunition, we were back on the road to continue the advance.

If we were lucky, sometime in mid afternoon we would stop long enough to get a can of cold rations into our growling stomachs. Roughly an hour before the daylight disappeared, we would move into a defensive position and immediately start digging our trench for the night.

This would be the only chance we had each day to actually get something hot to eat. Once the hole was down about two feet, my trench mate and I would immediately fire up one of our chemical heat blocks and try to warm up a canteen cup of water for coffee and a can of rations each. We had to be quick because once the daylight disappeared, any sources of light, including our tiny fire, had to be extinguished, lest we give away our position to the enemy. The odd person may have been fortunate enough to catch a hour or two of sleep, but most of us would spend the better part of the night patrolling the area, looking for enemy activity. As dawn broke the next day, the advance would begin anew.

You could almost feel the collective sigh of relief throughout the platoon when we finally heard the radio message announcing the end of the exercise.

By the time our course officer showed up, our kit had been checked and cleaned. All that remained was to wait for the truck transport to appear. Everywhere you looked people were smiling and happy to have made it through to the end. It was about twenty miles back to camp and the long-awaited hot shower, fresh food, and a warm bed.

We hadn't really seen much of our young course officer during the exercise. When he did appear, he rarely spoke to us. I don't remember his real name, because most of us referred to him as the "grim reaper." When a candidate failed in the performance of a leadership task, or simply wanted to quit, he was sent to see the grim reaper in the command vehicle. The hapless individual would collect all his personal kit and slowly head toward the back of the APC. After a few minutes, we could hear the hydraulics kick in, as the ramp was raised and the vehicle drove away, taking another training failure from the field.

On day one of the course, the staff had divided the 160 candidates into four separate platoons. When dawn broke on the final day of the field exercise, our original forty-man platoon was down to twenty-nine exhausted souls, which was about average throughout the battle school.

As the grim reaper appeared in front of the course that final morning, all the noisy chattered quickly subsided. We all waited for what we thought would be a few words of congratulations on passing the course. What came next was totally unexpected.

"This is the fourth course I have commanded and I must say that, without a doubt, you people are the absolute worst bunch of fucked up misfits I've ever had the misfortune to work with!" All the smiling faces quickly disappeared, and we stood there in stunned silence. "If I had my way, I'd fail the lot of you. Your performance during this test exercise was atrocious! As far as I am concerned, none of you have earned the right to ride back in a truck, so we are going to march back to base!"

Any joy we might have felt was long gone, as we tried to force our tired bodies to move forward and stay in step. We had gone less than half a mile and already I could feel the weight of my heavy wet rucksack digging into my shoulder blades. All around me I could hear the groans of pain, as each of us tried to muster up the last bit of strength we had. After we reached the main road, things got noticeably worse. At least the dirt track had been easier on our sore legs, but once we moved onto the hard asphalt, every step became torture on our blistered feet.

We had covered just over a mile, when the grim reaper spoke again. "Course halt!" Our drill certainly wasn't up to any kind of parade standard, as we all gingerly placed our feet down and came to a careful stop. "You people are a disgrace! Just look at you. We've only come a mile and already you're falling apart." As I looked around I knew he was wrong. We may have been exhausted, but based on the looks of hateful determination on each man's face, I knew we would all make it. We may be on our hands and knees for the last few steps, but this arrogant bastard wasn't about to make us quit.

"I would very much like to march you people right into the ground, but as the good sergeant has just reminded me, I can't force you to march if you are medically unfit. So, just around that corner there is one truck," he said, pointing down the road. "If any of you feels he cannot walk the whole distance, he can quit and get on the truck." It took a moment, but slowly someone in the rear rank raised his hand. "You ready to quit boy?" A smile of satisfaction filled the grim reaper's face.

"No sir," a defiant voice sounded from the back. "I don't want to walk back, sir. I'd rather march." A small ripple of laughter filled the ranks and for the first time, even the grim reaper smiled.

"Okay, gents. Now that's what I like to see. Sergeant, load them all on the trucks and I'll see you back at camp."

On the ride back to camp, I couldn't help but think about my good fortune during the exercise. I had been assessed in two command roles and managed to achieve high marks in each. Although I was quite happy with my marks, I could not help but wonder whether my success was the result of simple good luck or good leadership.

My first task had been to lead a five-man night reconnaissance patrol to scout a suspected enemy position. The target area was less than two miles away, over generally open ground. The entire process, start to finish, took about four hours. The next man scheduled for assessment had the much more difficult task of taking a twenty-man fighting patrol and attacking a position five miles away. Even though his patrol was much more difficult, the assessment criteria for both our tasks were identical.

My second command role in the field was one of those tasks that everyone hopes for.

The single most important factor in successfully passing any assessed task can be summed up in one simple word: *time.* The longer the instructor has to observe and assess your every move, the better your chances of screwing up. Near the end of the fourth day in the field, I was placed in command of the section while we continued the long advance. I knew there wasn't much daylight left as we moved down the road. I could only hope and pray that the enemy would open fire. Fortunately for me, I didn't have to wait long.

Once we heard the first shot, our section sprung into action. It took me just a few minutes to figure out where the enemy was and make my radio report to headquarters. Ten minutes later we were already moving around to the enemy's right flank in preparation for our final attack. After hurling some smoke grenades to cover our advance, we quickly overran the position and consolidated on the far side. The entire thing had taken about forty minutes, and I walked away with another solid passing mark.

By the time the instructor was done with me, it was already getting dark and we were about to go into a defensive position for the night. He turned to the next candidate and told him he was in charge of the section. I had been under assessment for a total of forty minutes, but the command ability of the poor unfortunate who followed me would be under continuous scrutiny for the next ten hours.

Much of the first few weeks in the battle school had been devoted to assessing our instructional ability. Although my initial efforts as a classroom and drill instructor had been barely good enough to get me selected for the course, by the time I gave my first lecture in the battle school, all of my earlier nervousness had completely disappeared. No longer did I dread the very thought of standing before a class full of students. I actually looked forward to the challenge of improving my grade with each successive lecture. After a steady progression of *B* grades, I finally managed a solid *A* on my final classroom lesson. Had I known what my reward would be for my little achievement, I might not have tried quite so hard.

The last few days of the course were devoted almost exclusively to graduation parade rehearsals. Despite our sore and blistered feet, the standard of drill slowly improved. Until then, I had been fortunate enough to make myself practically invisible in the rear rank. Unlike those in the front, I could at least make the odd mistake without being seen. All of that changed on the second last day.

All of the courses were standing around the edge of the square enjoying a much needed break after a solid ninety minutes of drill. It took a moment to register, but suddenly I heard the sergeant calling my name. "Burke, fall out and report to the school sergeant major," he shouted impatiently.

As I doubled toward the far end of the parade square, I could see there were already three candidates standing at attention before him.

So far on this course I had somehow managed to stay off his radar, but I was about to come face to face with the man we all called "the holy terror."

He may have been only five and a half feet tall, but when he shouted, his booming voice would resound across the entire camp. It was said that he could spot an errant drill movement from two hundred yards, and god help the man who fell under his watchful gaze. I once witnessed his verbal attack on a soldier who had made the unforgivable mistake of walking by a small piece of garbage without picking it up. The school sergeant major (SSM) was quick to demonstrate his ability to actually string a series of twenty or more curse words into one sentence and never repeat the same word twice. By the time he finished, his hapless victim was little more than a shivering mass of jelly.

"Well it's about bloody time," he shouted, as I came doubling into position. As soon as I slammed to a halt, he began to speak. I think we were all a little surprised by the unusual quiet tone of his voice. "Right, lads. You four are to be congratulated for coming first on your respective courses." He was actually smiling as he spoke. After taking a few moments to let that sink in, he spoke again, but in a much more business-like tone. "Each of you will be taking your platoon on parade, which means that you have until tomorrow to learn and memorize all the words of command." Once again he paused and stared at us each in turn. "Let me be perfectly clear, gentlemen. I not only expect you to do a good job, I demand it!"

When the big parade finally got underway, we actually looked quite good. Our long formation snaked its way along the edge of the road, through the entrance way, and across the front of the parade square. Being in charge of the lead platoon, my focus was on keeping our ranks marching straight as we continued along a thin, chalk line.

After all the stress and strain of rehearsal, the actual parade was rather anti-climatic. The commandant of the battle school made a long speech about the importance of the junior non-commissioned officer to the chain of command. By the time he got up to speak, we had already been standing stationary in the cold February wind for over an hour. He talked of the many changes which were about to overtake the rank system within the Canadian Forces, but all I could hear was the steady, low, muttered complaints of the guys shivering behind me. Had we not been so wimpy about the cold, perhaps we may have grasped the importance of his words.

• • •

By the spring of 1968, some huge changes to the military were already occurring. The Canadian Guards, the Queen's Own Rifles, and the Black Watch Regiment were all disappearing from the order of battle. The title of staff sergeant had been eliminated and replaced by the new rank of warrant officer. The rank of lance corporal was slowly being phased out, but it would be a few months before the new rank of master corporal was created. Although the ranks of corporal and sergeant still existed, the duties and responsibilities of these ranks had both been significantly downgraded. Even the officer ranks of lieutenant and captain were not immune to changes in their status.

Like the vast majority of rank and file soldiers, I thought that our new minister of national defence, Paul Hellyer, was just another politician trying to make his mark at the military's expense. Even after a number of generals, admirals, and colonels resigned in protest, our political masters continued to push forward with their changes to the system.

I may have had less than five years in the army, but even I could see that the infantry platoon, the most basic component of the army, was slowly being eroded.

For hundreds of years, the infantry platoon was commanded by a lieutenant, with a sergeant as his second in command. The three ten-man sections within the platoon were each run by a corporal. Although the composition had not changed, the post-1968 platoon was commanded by a lieutenant or a captain. The second in command became a warrant officer, and the three sections were each controlled by a sergeant. The experience level of the platoon may have increased tenfold, but most of the people involved in the initial changes found the new system rather degrading.

A captain who had previously helped run a company of 150 men was relegated to commanding a platoon of thirty. A sergeant who had overseen a platoon of thirty, then commanded a section of just ten. The poor corporal who had once controlled a full section became little more than a well-trained private.

It would take a few years to sort itself out, but unfortunately by the time it did, many of the more experienced and senior members had already left in disgust.

• • •

We had been back to work in the battalion for about two weeks when the six top students from our course got the call to report to the CO's office. Unlike our predecessors, who had waited for months or even years, we had walked into the colonel's office as private soldiers and left, five minutes later, with two hooks and the rank of full corporal.

Walking into the corporals' mess for the very first time that night was quite an intimidating experience. The entire room was silent while the six of us stood awkwardly waiting for someone, anyone, to acknowledge our presence. It would have been easy to just turn around and walk out, but that would have only postponed the inevitable. Like it or not, we had become members of the corporals' mess and would somehow have to get through this. Without a doubt, the most difficult people to face were the few remaining lance corporals, who, for whatever reason, still maintained their old rank. Lance Corporal Wilfang sat near the window, holding his mug of beer and just glaring in our direction. His hostile look said it all. This guy had been through the Korean War. Now here we were, standing in the doorway, a bunch of snot-nosed kids, each with two hooks. None of us had ever seen a shoot fired in anger, but we all outranked him.

After a few moments of being ignored, we headed for the bar in the far corner of the room. Even with my back to the crowd, I could still feel their hostile glances burning holes in the back of my head.

Unfortunately, it took a very long time for us to finally glean even the slightest amount of respect from the remainder of the battalion. Regardless of how conscientiously we did our duties in garrison or how well we performed in the field, many still refused to refer to us simply by our rank, but in the much more derogatory term of "Hellyer's Corporals."

Epilogue
A House Is Not a Home

I was more than a little apprehensive as I made my way up the road toward the Catholic chapel. A steady, unrelenting rain had been pelting the camp all morning. Even though I held the collar of my raincoat tightly at the neck, I could still feel the odd rain drop seeping through the edges of the material. But while January rain may have been biting and cold, I hardly noticed it. My mind was somewhere else.

Just a few months earlier, I had taken this same walk to see the Padre. The news had been bad then and I knew it was going to be even worse now. When a soldier is told to report to the Padre, he can be sure that the news is never good, but at least on that first visit I had held out some faint hope that perhaps he had mixed me up with someone else in the battalion.

I actually felt a little sorry for the Padre. It can't be easy when you are always the bearer of bad news. His facial features were appropriately sad as he sat me down to break the news about my father.

My father had been diagnosed with cancer and placed in a sanatorium hospital some months earlier. According to my sister's letters, his condition had stabilized for a long period, but as the Padre had explained on my first visit, things were deteriorating rapidly.

After leaving the Padre's office, I picked up my leave pass from the battalion orderly room, and within minutes I was on my way to Dusseldorf Airport for the long flight home.

Thankfully by the time I arrived at the sanatorium in St. Catharines, Ontario, his condition had once again stabilized. According to the doctors he was never going to get better, but at least for the moment he wasn't in imminent danger. I spent the next few days travelling back and forth to the hospital, but could do nothing more than sit and watch him slip in and out of consciousness. I had hoped that he and I could talk, but we never got the opportunity. Once or twice he did speak, but he didn't know who I was. He called me Billy, thinking I was my older brother over from Ireland. I knew it was no good trying to explain, so I just played along, in the role of Billy, for what was to be our final brief conversation.

After just a week of compassionate leave, I returned to Germany, knowing full well that it was only a matter of time before the next call came from the Padre.

My mood may have been sombre throughout the long plane ride back to Germany, but that all changed when I saw Brigitte's smile when I walked through the front door of our tiny apartment. Even though Brigitte had known the day before I left for Canada, she had decided that her news was best kept until I returned. We were going to have a second child.

Eric was almost two weeks old before I got to see him for the very first time. Moments after his birth, he had been rushed to another hospital some thirty miles away after a blood clot was discovered near his brain. After a four-hour operation and a month or more of uncertainty, we were finally allowed to take him home. Although the doctors told us he was out of danger, Brigitte and I still took turns standing vigil over his crib each night. He must have been at least three months old before we both finally relaxed enough to sleep through the night.

When I arrived in the chapel for my second visit that rainy January morning, the Padre confirmed my worst fears. My father had passed away in his sleep the night before. The doctors told me later that on top of the cancer, he had suddenly contracted pneumonia and his system was just too weak to fight both infections. The cause of death may have been clinically correct, but I always believed that there are illnesses that cannot be seen or treated by medical science. Cancer and pneumonia may have brought about my father's death, but his zest for life had left him the day my mother died, seven years earlier.

Maybe things could have been different. Maybe I could have been different. That thought has plagued me my entire life. I could have tried to see things from his perspective. To suddenly find yourself alone with nine kids must have been devastating. Instead of trying to understand his reality, my continuous bad behaviour simply added to his problems.

The thought had often crossed my mind that the reason we didn't get along was because we were more alike than either of us was willing to admit. He had rebelled against a strict upbringing and run away to join the army at the age sixteen. I like to believe that if he had met my new wife and babies, and if he could have seen that I was finding my way in the life, that he would have been proud and happy for me.

All of these things ran through my mind as I left the Padre's office and headed up the road to once again pick up a leave pass for the trip home.

The once weekly flight from Dusseldorf had departed the day before, so my only remaining option was to try and reach the Canadian Air Force base in Marvel, France. After thirty hours and numerous transfers at every major rail centre in Germany, Luxembourg, and France, I made it to the airport with little time to spare. My two-and-a-half-day odyssey ended with my arrival in Toronto just hours before my father's funeral.

It had been a very long time since I had voluntarily stepped inside a Catholic church, but that didn't stop me from offering an earnest prayer for my father. I may have had a difficult time deciding whether to believe or not, but I knew that my father did and that's all that really mattered. I prayed that what the priests had told us since early childhood was true. I prayed that there was a heaven and that my father was there and finally reunited with my mother.

Even though I had only been gone for four years, already I could see there had been many subtle changes to all that I used to find so familiar.

My last day home was spent wandering through our old east-end neighbourhood, but after hours of searching for familiar faces, I left with a great sense of emptiness. I think it was Thomas Wolfe who said, "You can never go home again." I had read his book, *Look Homeward Angel,* years earlier, but never truly understood the meaning of the phrase until that day spent walking past my old school, through Riverdale Park, down Parliament Street, and along Gerrard Street. I stood gazing at our old home in the narrow laneway of Dermott Place. What had once been a home full of life and noisy kids was now just an abandoned, empty shell of a house. All the familiar landmarks were there, but somehow it was different. When I walked into the Satellite Restaurant, I half expected to see my old friends, Harold and Donny, sitting and waiting for me to show up, but there was nothing there for me anymore. Four years ago I had felt comfortable in these surroundings, but today I just felt a great sense of unease. I didn't belong here anymore.

When I had passed through Toronto on my way to Germany back in 1965, I truly believed that this was the home I'd return to someday. As I departed the city a week after the funeral, I just knew that everything had changed for me. My family was still very close to each other, but I no longer felt part of that life. I knew that the picture-perfect future that had filled my mind's eye for all those years growing up was never going to be a reality. I may return from time to time, but this place would never be my home again.

• • •

Over the next forty years, the majority of my time would be spent outside of Canada. By the time we left Germany after a second lengthy tour, my son and daughter were already into their teenage years. Long after they had grown and gone off to start their own adult lives, Brigitte and I were still traipsing about the Middle East, on what would be my ninth tour as a United Nations military observer.

Sure there were times, especially late at night, when I would think about Canada. Sitting alone in an observation post in the Sinai Desert, or on a hillside in South Lebanon, your mind can't help but ponder the life choices you've made. When people would ask me if I missed Canada, my immediate answer would be yes. Certainly I missed turning on a tap and being able to drink the water. I missed being able to drive down a road without wearing a flak jacket for fear of a roadside bomb. But, most of all, I missed living in a country with four distinct and separate seasons.

I missed Canada for many reasons, but not because I thought of it as home. Whether we were living in a tiny two-room flat in downtown Soest, a fourth-floor walk up in Damascus, Syria, or a house on the Lebanese border, we always felt at home, at least for that moment in time.

After all, a house may be some place to live, but a home is really just a state of mind.

Of Related Interest

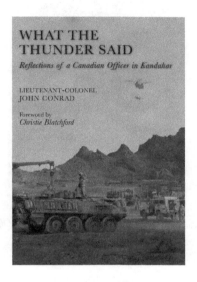

What the Thunder Said
Reflections of a Canadian Officer in Kandahar
by Lieutenant-Colonel John Conrad

978-1554884087
$29.95, £17.99

By every principle of war, every shred of military logic, logistics support to Canada's Task Force Orion in Afghanistan should have collapsed in July 2006. There are few countries that offer a greater challenge to logistics than Afghanistan, and yet Canadian soldiers lived through an enormous test on this deadly international stage — a monumental accomplishment. *What the Thunder Said* is an honest, raw recollection of incidents and impressions of Canadian war-fighting from a logistics perspective. It offers solid insight into the history of military logistics in Canada and explores in some detail the dramatic erosion of a once-proud corner of the army from the perspective of a battalion commander.

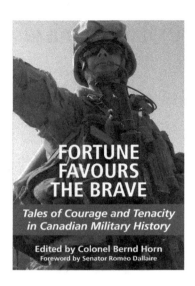

Fortune Favours the Brave
Tales of Courage and Tenacity in Canadian Military History
by Colonel Bernd Horn

978-1550028416
$35.00, £20.00

As U.S. Secretary of State Condoleezza Rice has commented, "Canadians are fierce fighters." *Fortune Favours the Brave* certainly proves this point in a collection of essays that showcases the fighting spirit and courage of Canada's military. The daring actions featured in this book range from the cat-and-mouse struggle between Canadian partisans and Rogers's Rangers in the Seven Years' War in the 1750s, to an innovative trench raid in the First World War, the valiant parachute assault to penetrate the Third Reich in the Second World War, covert submarine operations during the Cold War, and Operation Medusa in Afghanistan.

Available at your favourite bookseller.

What did you think of this book?
Visit *www.dundurn.com* for reviews, videos, updates, and more!